W9-BUS-691

MARTYN COX

Wildlife Gardening

LONDON, NEW YORK,
MELBOURNE, MUNICH, and DELHI

Senior designer Sonia Whillock-Moore
Senior editors Deborah Lock, Elinor Greenwood
Designers Hedi Hunter, Sadie Thomas,
Clemence de Molliens, Natalie Godwin, Lauren Rosier
Photography Will Heap, Caroline Hughes
Picture researcher Jo Walton
RHS consultant Simon Maughan

Category publisher Mary Ling
Production editor Clare McLean
Production controller Claire Pearson
Jacket designer Hedi Hunter
Jacket editor Mariza O'Keeffe
Jacket copywriter Adam Powley
US editor Margaret Parrish

First published in the United States in 2009 by
DK Publishing
375 Hudson Street, New York, New York 10014
in association with The Royal Horticultural Society, UK
www.rhs.org.uk

09 10 11 12 13 10 9 8 7 6 5 4 3 2 1
RD172 – 01/09

A catalog record for this book
is available from the Library of Congress
ISBN 978-0-7566-5089-6

Printed and bound by Toppan, China

Contents

Foreword

For many people, attracting wildlife into the garden means putting out food for the birds. And this is as good a place to start as any! But you can easily take your interest further—it really doesn't take much to transform your garden into a haven for all kinds of birds, bugs, amphibians, reptiles, and mammals. All you need is a little know-how!

Any garden, however large or small, can be turned into a wildlife sanctuary using the activities in this book. You can fill it with the right plants, provide animals with food, and build them special habitats, whether it's a pond, bog, nesting site, or somewhere they can hibernate over the long winter months.

This book is filled with planting ideas, along with step-by-step instructions. All of the activities are easy to do and won't take long—many can even be done without the help of an adult! And, after you've transformed your garden, you'll find all the tips, tricks, and advice you'll need to help you record, identify, and track down wildlife.

There are so many reasons why it's worth it to become a wildlife gardener. Many creatures are rare and need a helping hand to survive, while others are simply fascinating to watch. A healthy population of wildlife is also good for the garden: bugs pollinate plants, worms eat garbage, and frogs and birds devour creatures that we consider to be pests.

So, what are you waiting for? Head outside, start your wildlife garden, and you'll be amazed at just how many creatures you'll find outside your back door.

Martyn Cox

Guide to symbols

Ask an adult for help

Grow it: Activities for growing plants for wildlife

Make it: Activities for making habitats that encourage wildlife

Watch it: Activities for watching and observing wildlife

Top 10: Plants for wildlife

These symbols show the conditions the plants prefer as a planting guide.

Prefers a sunny or slightly sheltered place

Height plant grows to

Prefers a place in direct sunlight

Grows in well-drained soil

Grows in moist soil

Grows in wet soil

Find out more

The American Horticultural Society is one of the nation's oldest gardening societies. Its mission is to educate and inspire people to become successful, environmentally responsible gardeners. It's never too young to start: check out the youth gardening section, and find out about local gardening organizations and activities. Now, start digging!

For more information and to join, contact:
American Horticultural Society
7931 East Boulevard Drive
Alexandria, VA 22308
Tel. 1-800-777-7931
www.ahs.org

Why be a wildlife gardener?

Nature is amazing. And it is especially exciting to see plants and animals flourish in a beautiful wildlife garden created by YOU. Creatures will visit your garden with only a little encouragement and by helping them, they help you. Garden animals work hard to keep your garden colorful and healthy—just how they, and you, like it.

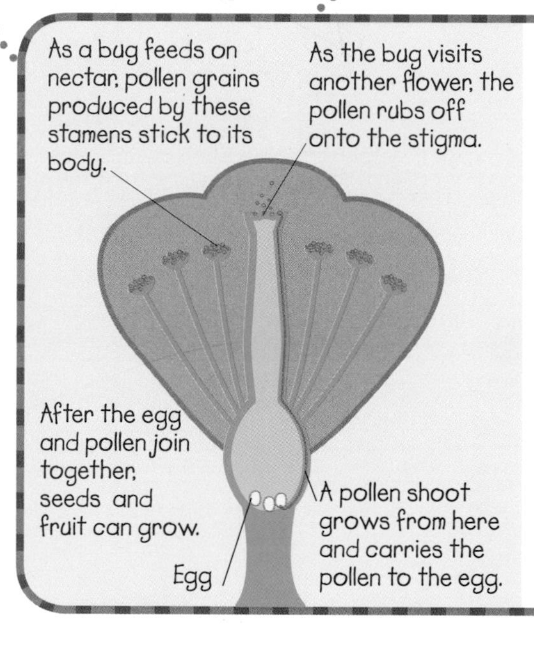

Flower power

Providing a home for bees, butterflies, and other nectar-drinking bugs is important since they are pollinators. Without them, insect-pollinated flowering plants would not exist as they transfer pollen (fine grains) from the male part of a flower to the female part, so seeds can be made and the next generation of plants grow.

Sow the seed

Encouraging different animals and birds helps spread plant seeds far and wide. Some seeds have sticky or spiked coats that get caught on the fur of an animal brushing past. Other seeds are found inside tasty fruit. After animals have eaten the fruit, these seeds are spread in their droppings.

Superworms

Worms love gardeners' well-dug soil and in return make the soil healthy for growing plants. These incredible creatures eat decaying plant matter, which passes through their bodies and is deposited as a nutrient-rich cast (poop) near the surface. Their underground tunneling also improves drainage and allows air into the soil—all a big help to plants.

Pest control

And we're not talking about your little brother! There are a lot of creatures that can cause damage in the garden, but by providing a home for a variety of wildlife you can create a natural balance. Ladybugs and lacewings love to eat aphids, while spiders will catch mosquitoes and flying pests in their webs. Blue tits devour caterpillars, thrushes like snails, and toads enjoy eating their slippery partners-in-crime, slugs.

It's fun!

Wildlife gardening is fun, fascinating, and exciting! Watching birds on a feeder, a squirrel scampering across the lawn, or newts diving in a pond is even more satisfying if you know you helped to provide it all.

Your garden is a habitat

Whether they are big, small, or microscopic; live in water, soil, or in the branches of a tree, from the cutest mammal to the creepiest bug, animals need each other. There is a great interaction between all living creatures and by turning your garden into a haven for wildlife, you are helping to preserve a well-balanced, self-sustaining environment. AND you are helping to preserve North America's natural heritage. It's all good!

Food web

Here's a food web that might exist in anyone's garden. Remember, even the creatures you may not like provide food for other animals.

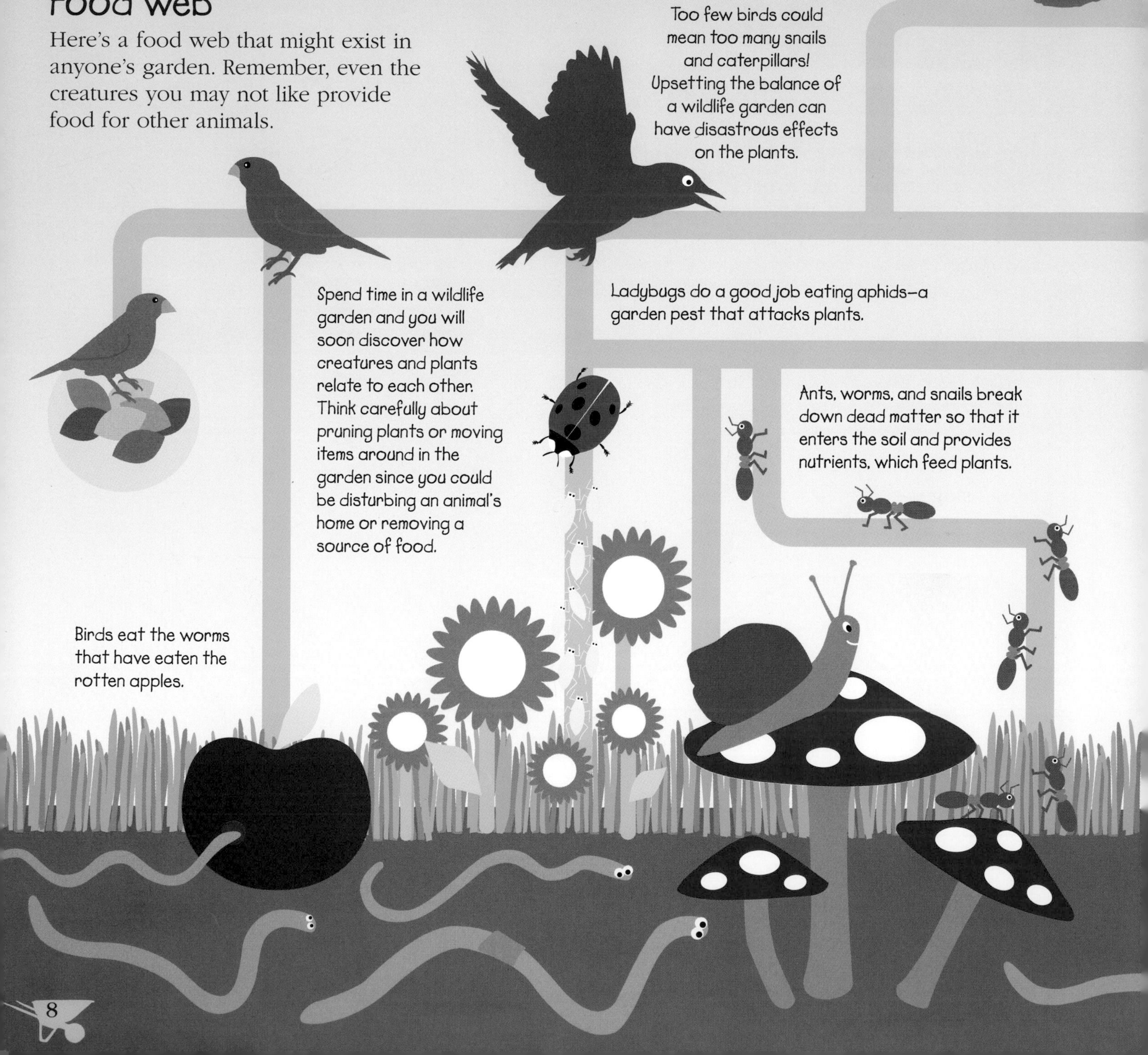

Too few birds could mean too many snails and caterpillars! Upsetting the balance of a wildlife garden can have disastrous effects on the plants.

Spend time in a wildlife garden and you will soon discover how creatures and plants relate to each other. Think carefully about pruning plants or moving items around in the garden since you could be disturbing an animal's home or removing a source of food.

Ladybugs do a good job eating aphids–a garden pest that attacks plants.

Ants, worms, and snails break down dead matter so that it enters the soil and provides nutrients, which feed plants.

Birds eat the worms that have eaten the rotten apples.

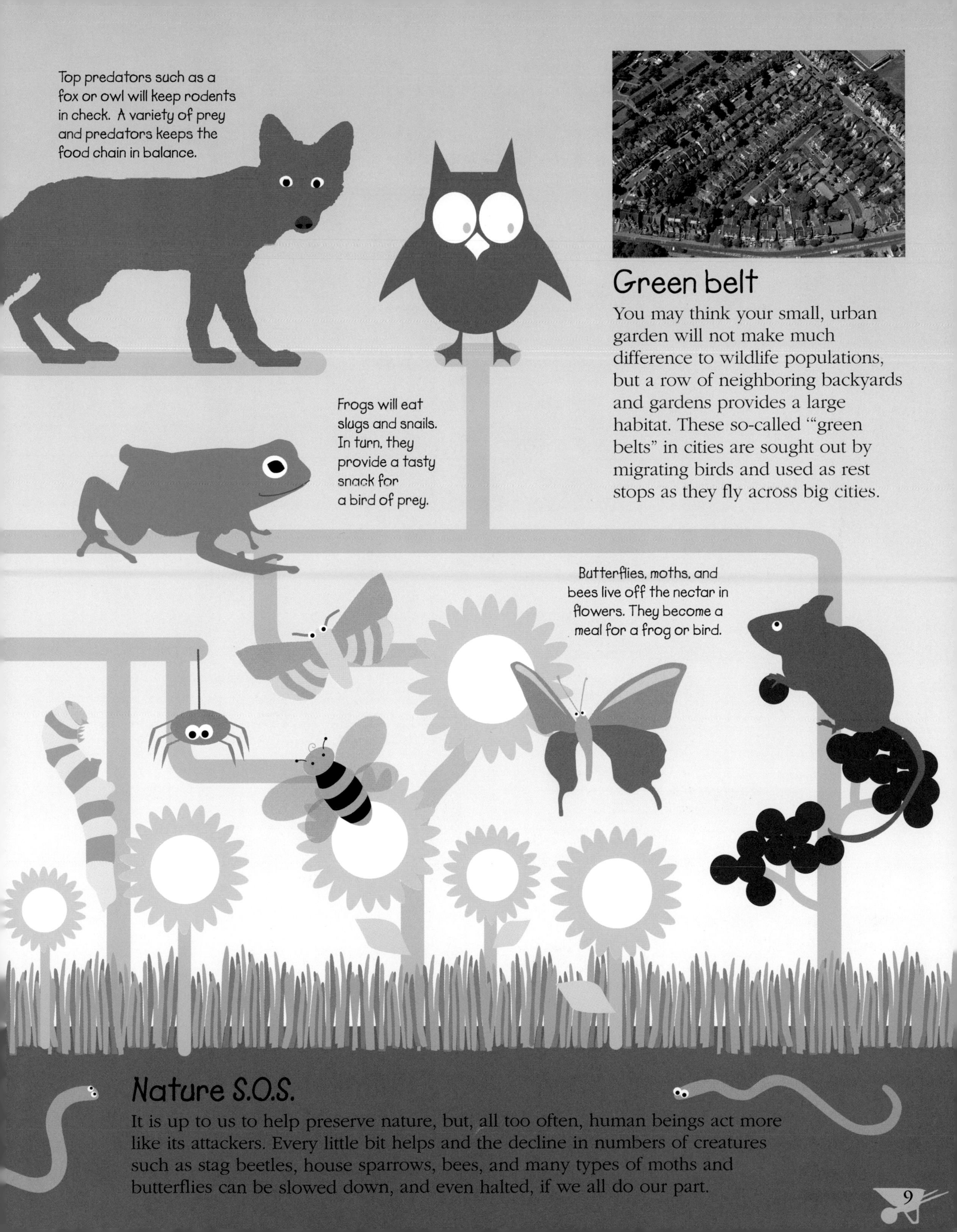

Top predators such as a fox or owl will keep rodents in check. A variety of prey and predators keeps the food chain in balance.

Frogs will eat slugs and snails. In turn, they provide a tasty snack for a bird of prey.

Butterflies, moths, and bees live off the nectar in flowers. They become a meal for a frog or bird.

Green belt

You may think your small, urban garden will not make much difference to wildlife populations, but a row of neighboring backyards and gardens provides a large habitat. These so-called '“green belts” in cities are sought out by migrating birds and used as rest stops as they fly across big cities.

Nature S.O.S.

It is up to us to help preserve nature, but, all too often, human beings act more like its attackers. Every little bit helps and the decline in numbers of creatures such as stag beetles, house sparrows, bees, and many types of moths and butterflies can be slowed down, and even halted, if we all do our part.

Wildlife gardening—the basics

To create a fabulous wildlife garden, follow the activities in this section. You can learn to plant a tree, put in a pond, plant up a window box, and start composting. These general activities will form the basis of your wildlife garden and soon your outside space—whatever its size—will be buzzing, crawling, flying, and hopping with all kinds of amazing creatures.

Grow it

p. 24

Grow some sunflowers

Make it

p. 14

Put in a pond

Watch it

p. 28

Keep a nature diary

p. 18 Grow it
Plant a tree
p. 22 Make it
Start composting
p. 26 Grow it
Plant a window box
p. 17 Make it
Hibernation log pile

Top 10

Start-up plants

So, you've got a patio or garden, and you want to start wildlife gardening. What should you plant? There are thousands of plants to choose from, and here's our top ten to get you started. This mixture of flowers, trees, climbers, and shrubs will be a magnet to wildlife and will make an ideal basis to your wildlife garden. In addition to ornamental plants, which are known to be irresistible to wildlife, include plenty of native plants in your planting plan.

1

Wildflowers

Native wildflowers are the favorite food plants for our indigenous wildlife. There are hundreds to choose from, but pick plants that grow naturally in your area.

- Sunny or partly shaded location
- Well drained, moist soil
- Grows 24 in (60 cm) high

2

Clematis

(C. tangutica)

Any type of clematis is popular with wildlife, and this variety, with its golden lantern shaped-flowers and fluffy seed heads that last well into winter, is a climber that is bushy enough for birds to nest in.

- Sunny location
- Well drained soil
- Grows 22 ft (7 m) high

3

Butterfly bush

(Buddleia davidii)

It's all in the name with this beautiful bush. This is a wildlife garden "must-have," with its long clusters of scented flowers—a favorite stop-off for bees and butterflies. Birds will flock to it, too, to gobble up small insects.

- Sunny location
- Well drained soil
- Grows 6-7 ft (2 m) high

4

Dog rose

(Rosa canina)

This scrambling rose is supported by other plants, often in a native hedge. It has stunning pink flowers and the branches are clothed in beautiful red hips during the fall.

- Sunny or partly shaded location
- Well drained, moist soil
- Grows 9 ft (3 m) high

5

Long grass

A patch of ornamental grass that has been left to grow long will do wonders for wildlife. Birds will gather material for nests, beetles and insects will use it as cover, and ladybugs will hibernate among long tufts.

- Sunny or partly shaded location
- Well drained soil
- Grows 40 in (1 m) high

6

Common ivy

(Hedera helix)

An evergreen climber, ivy can be grown against walls or fences, where it will provide shelter and cover for birds—some may even nest in it. A flourishing population of insects and spiders will take up residence, too.

- Sunny or partly shaded location
- Well drained, moist soil
- Grows 33 ft (10 m) high

7 French lavender

(Lavandula stoechas)

Bees and butterflies love the showy spikes of aromatic flowers that top this evergreen. Its leaves have a scent, too, in summer. English lavender (*Lavandula angustifolia*) is also a good choice and is a hardier plant.

- Sunny location
- Well drained soil
- Grows 24 in (60 cm) high

8 Ornamental crab apple (Malus)

A large group of trees with blossom in the spring, followed by clusters of jewel-like fruit. The foliage of many is stunning in the fall, too. Choose a tree that's the right size for your garden.

- Sunny or partly shaded location
- Well drained, moist soil
- Grows 13–40 ft (4–12 m) high

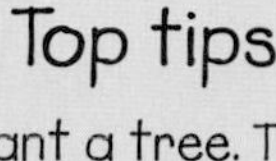

Top tips

- Plant a tree. These provide a perch for birds and will bring them flocking.
- Plant wildflowers. They are great for bugs.

9 Birch tree

(Betula pendula 'Youngii')

Many birches are towering, but Young's weeping birch has a weeping stance, making it a much better choice for smaller gardens.

- Sunny or partly shaded location
- Well drained, moist soil
- Grows 26 ft (8 m) high

10 Mixed native hedge

Hazel, field maple, holly, alder, dogwood, spindle, hawthorn, blackthorn, and European privet

A boundary of mixed native shrubs and trees will be full of wildlife. The network of branches provide nesting sites for birds, the flowers attract insects, and many of the plants boast berries or nuts that will be eaten by many creatures. Some wildlife will hibernate in the leaves that gather beneath the hedge.

- Sunny or partly shaded location
- Well drained, moist soil
- Grows 3–6 ft (1–2 m) high

What's an annual?

Annuals are usually the most colorful plants that you see when looking for new plants. They live for one season only and then they die. Plant them into your garden when they are full of buds.

What's a perennial?

Perennial plants flower or grow back year after year. After their blooming season, they die back or become dormant (asleep) for the winter. These make a good foundation for your garden.

What's an evergreen?

An evergreen is like its name suggests–its leaves are always green. These make good cover for creatures all year round.

Top tips

If you have a lawn, **make a meadow.** Just let a patch of grass grow long.

Make a wildlife pond. Even an upturned trash can lid provides a place for creatures to drink and bathe in.

Make it

Pond life

Like us, animals need to drink water to survive, and they like somewhere to bathe, too. Aside from being a drinking hole, even a very small pond will quickly become alive with water bugs and other aquatic creatures. Adding pond plants will provide food and cover—the perfect habitat for frogs and toads.

Putting in a pond

• Be safe! Near water, young children need adult supervision at all times.

• A pond is best positioned in semi-shade. Some sunlight will help plants to grow, but too much will promote the growth of algae.

• Avoid windswept places since these will put off wildlife and cause pond water to evaporate quickly.

• Position your pond away from trees to avoid spending time removing leaves from the water.

• Make your pond in longer grass, which will give creatures cover around the pond. Piles of loose stones or a log pile placed near the edge will give amphibians somewhere to hide.

What you will need:

1

Mark out the pond's boundary by turning your plastic container upside down and trickling sand around the edges.

4

Cover the edge of the pond and the rim of the container with the flat stones or slabs. Cover the bottom with gravel, then place the bricks or large stones inside the container to make different levels within the pond.

5

Take the water plants and cover their soil with gravel to stop them from floating away. See pages 54-55 for some plant ideas. Position the pots inside the pond, on a large stone if necessary.

Aftercare tips

Clear fallen leaves from the pond. These will rot and pollute the water.

Float a tennis ball on the surface of the pond so if the water freezes there will be an air hole. Do not shatter frozen ice since this shocks the creatures living below.

If floating weed gets out of hand, pull some out. Then leave it overnight next to the pond before throwing it away, so creatures living in it can crawl back into the water.

2 **Dig all around the boundary first** (marked out by the sand), then dig out the middle, making a hole deep enough for the container.

3 **Place the container into the hole** so the top is level with the ground. Fill any gaps with soil.

6 **Fill the pond** with water and add free floating pond weed. Make a ramp for creatures to climb in and out by covering a piece of wood with wire mesh. In hot weather, refill the pond with rainwater.

7 **Over the next few months**, especially in the summer, pond insects will take up residence or lay eggs.

Watch it

Your seasonal wildlife garden

The amount of wildlife in your garden varies with the seasons. Spring is when you are most likely to see baby animals. Summer is abuzz with wildlife. Fall is when animals make the most of the harvest bounty, and winter is a quiet time when many animals hibernate.

Spring

Wake up! It's springtime. So get busy! As warm weather arrives, frogs, toads, and newts, and spiders wake up from hibernation. Birds find mates, make nests, and lay eggs, while later in the season frogs and toads release their spawn into ponds.

Summer

The warm, sunny days of summer mean lots of food for wildlife. Butterflies flit between flowers, fledgling birds take to the air, and bees work tirelessly to produce honey. Baby frogs and toads can be spotted in ponds, while dragonflies dart across the water.

Make a hibernation log pile

MAKE IT

A log pile is a welcome place to rest for animals and insects looking for somewhere to hibernate. They can hide among the cracks, really wedging themselves in, and go to sleep. So get busy building this hibernation log pile in an undisturbed corner—and leave it undisturbed, at least until spring is well underway.

Fall

In the fall, spiders put on amazing displays of webs, while a feast of berries and fruit on trees attract masses of birds, giving them the chance to fatten up before winter. Squirrels bury nuts for eating later. By mid-fall some creatures will be looking for a place to sleep out the winter.

Winter

This is the quiet time, and when animals most need our help. Birds are extremely vulnerable in winter and need high-energy food and water to help them survive the cold, lean months ahead.

What you will need:

Shovel

Logs and sticks

Bark, leaves, and an ivy plant.

1

Dig a very shallow pit in a shady, undisturbed place. Pile up the logs, with the biggest logs at the bottom, in the pit.

2

Pile up the smaller sticks on top, criss-crossing them. Fill any spaces with bark, stones, pinecones, and leaves.

3

Plant an ivy and trail over the log pile.

Grow it: Plant a tree

Every wildlife garden should have at least one tree. Leafy canopies provide shelter for timid creatures, while birds and some small mammals will build nests in their branches. Berries, fruit, and nuts are an important source of food, and blossoms attract pollinating insects. Choose your trees carefully. Some are ideal in a small space, but others are more suitable for a larger garden.

What you will need:

Shovel

A tree—crab apple is a good choice

Stake

Rubber tree tie

Watering can

1 **First dig your hole.** Make the hole at least twice as wide as the tree's "rootbase."

2 **Make sure it's the right depth** by placing a stick across the hole and seeing if it is level with the tree's container.

3 **Remove the plastic** around the tree's roots and fill in the soil around the tree.

4 **Hammer in your stake** at a 45° angle and tie the stake to the tree with a tree tie.

5 **Water the tree.** Job complete! Make sure you keep the tree well watered and remove the stake when the tree is strong enough to stand alone.

Tree life

The mammal you are most likely to see in a tree is a squirrel. They love nuts and fruits, and are extremely acrobatic. They sleep in it, eat in it, and they like playing in it, too!

A tree that blossoms in spring provides a nectar feast for bees and other insects. In fact, fruit trees rely on insects for pollination. If it weren't for bugs, there would be no fruit.

Birds eat berries and fruit from trees. The fall glut provides them with enough food to help get through winter.

TREE IN A POT

Planting a tree in a pot is just as easy. Make sure there is a hole in the bottom of the pot, covered with a layer of pebbles. Place your tree in the center and fill in with loam-based compost (which is the best at holding water and will keep the tree upright).

Grow it

A wildlife hedge

Hedges are alive with wildlife. They provide food, shelter, cover, security, and a place for animals to hibernate and raise their young. Not only that, but as a hedge flowers, it also attracts a mass of buzzing, nectar-eating bees, butterflies, and bugs.

What makes a native hedge?

A native hedge is composed of several different trees and shrubs, climbers, and wildflowers. Typically, it will consist of 25 percent hawthorn and then four other varieties of tree. After it is established, native climbing plants and wildflowers can be added. Among the best trees and shrubs are spindle, hazel, field maple, sweet briar, crabapple, blackthorn, and common alder. Honeysuckle, ivy, and clematis are ideal climbers. And, to make it even more wildlife-friendly, you could plant wild primrose, wild strawberry, red campion, and chickweed at the bottom.

Sparrow

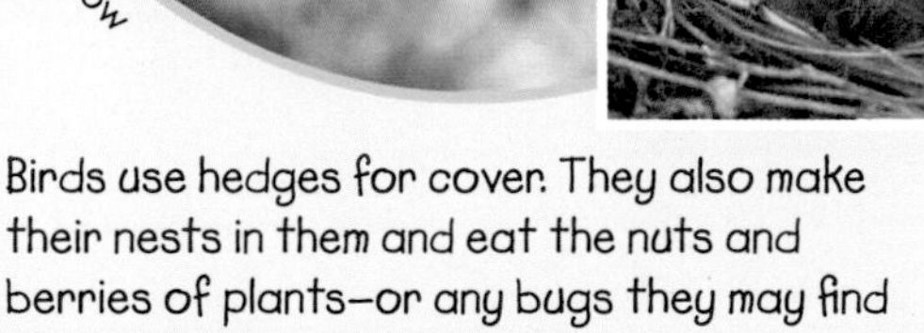

Birds use hedges for cover. They also make their nests in them and eat the nuts and berries of plants—or any bugs they may find there, as this sparrow is doing.

Mice like to live in hedgerows. They are agile and can climb to the upper branches of hedges. They are on the lookout for snails, centipedes, and other tasty creatures to munch on.

Insects feed and live on plants. They also make a tasty snack for birds. Many are well camouflaged to blend into their green background and are hard to spot, even when you are looking right at them!

Bees and butterflies are attracted by the nectar-rich flowers that grow on some hedges, like the hawthorn. They also like the flowers that grow at the base of hedges.

Voles shelter at the bottom of a hedge and use its protection to move from one part of the garden to another. These shy creatures are difficult to see since they only come out at night and like to stay hidden.

Frogs and toads hibernate in old wood that gathers at the bottom of the hedge. They can also feed on any passing bugs during the summer, camouflaging beautifully into the leaf litter at the base.

Grow your own hedge

A hedge looks great around a garden or yard. Trees and shrubs are best planted in the fall, spaced 1 ft (36 cm) apart. If you don't have the room to plant one, you can grow an ornamental hedge in a long, wide container such as a trough. Fill it with all-purpose compost and place plants close together. Let them knit together. Keep plants at a manageable height by pruning. They will soon attract lots of insects and pollinators.

Make it Continue composting

Many people use artificial pesticides or fertilizers, but it is better for wildlife to avoid the use of unnatural substances, as they can upset a garden's natural balance. Use homemade compost to improve your soil and make a fabulous habitat for wildlife at the same time—your compost bin!

Scraps of food and paper slowly rot and turn into rich compost. Put it in a pot, add a seed, sun, and water, and WOW!

Compost critters

Not only is composting a great way to recycle waste that may end up in a landfill, but it also provides a habitat for a web of compost creatures. It is amazing how quickly animals colonize a place they like. They can get in through surprisingly small nooks and crannies. Here is some of the wildlife you might find in a compost heap.

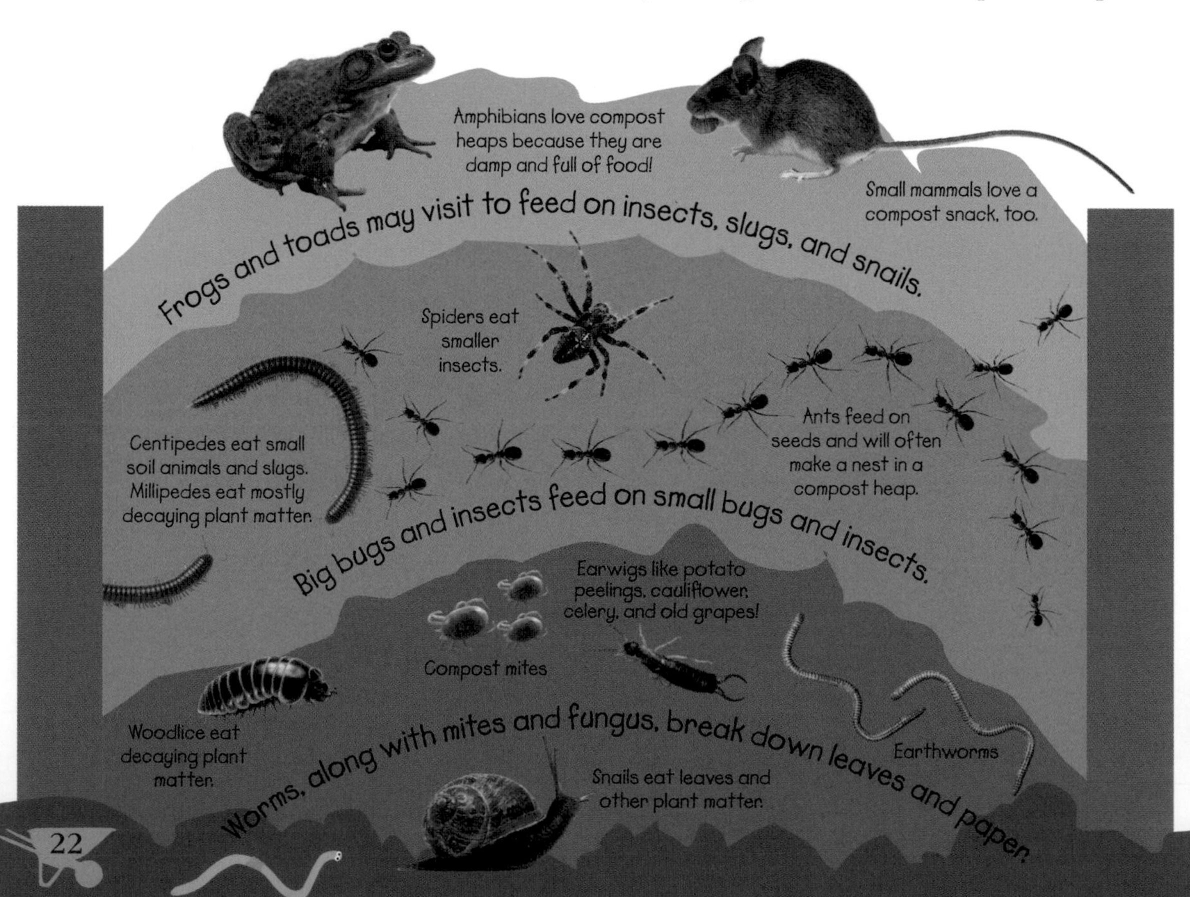

Home composting

Composting is the ultimate in recycling and it is great for your garden. Rather than putting plant waste in the garbage, it is added to a compost bin where it will warm up and rot down. This can then be dug into the soil, where its goodness helps plants to grow healthily, or spread across the surface to suppress weeds and hold in moisture—this will eventually be mixed into the soil by earthworms. Many tiny creatures live on decaying plant matter and larger ones feed on them, so composting helps to keep the food chain in balance.

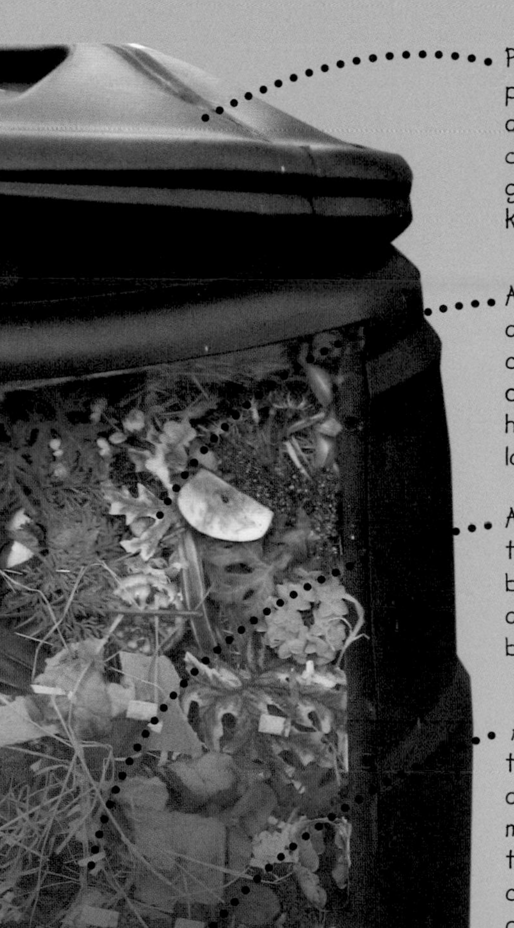

Put your bin in a sunny place on top of soil, not concrete, so water can drain out and bugs can get in. Cover the bin to keep heat in and rain out.

At the top, your compost will be green and fresh. Every month or so, ask an adult to help you mix the top layers with a fork.

After 12 weeks or more, the compost will start to break down and change color and texture as the bugs do their work.

About 20 weeks later, the waste is becoming compost. It has been munched to pieces by thousands of creatures and is very hot in the center.

Your reward... nice, rich compost!

Sorting it out

Your waste can generally be split into two groups: the greens and the browns. The greens are soft, sappy material that rots quickly and provides nitrogen and moisture to the mix.

The browns are drier materials that are rich in carbon, providing fiber and giving compost its structure. On their own, greens would produce a foul-smelling sludge, so it's important to include more browns than greens.

- Dead heads of flowers
- Leaves
- Grass clippings
- Plant clippings
- Tea bags
- Coffee grounds
- Annual weeds
- Dried perennial weeds
- Broken egg shells
- Vegetable peelings
- Apple cores
- Fruit peels
- Shredded newspaper
- Shredded cardboard

No

- Animal waste
- Cat litter
- Meat
- Fish
- Bread
- Metal
- Plastic
- Cooked food
- Diseased plant material
- Fresh perennial weeds
- Invasive perennial weeds such as bindweed and Japanese knotweed
- Glossy magazine paper

Grow it

Smiley sunflowers

Sunflowers are great all-arounders for wildlife, and if you have room for just one plant, make it a sunflower! They grow well in any large container—just make sure they have plenty of water and sunlight. These plants are not only easy and fun to grow, reaching amazing heights, but they also provide year-round food for wildlife.

Bright yellow petals attract insects

This is where the seeds grow—a favorite snack for birds.

The tallest sunflower ever grown was 25 ft (7.76 m) tall.

Did you know?

- Sunflowers are not only yellow. Seed companies sell varieties with white, orange, red, and chocolate colored blooms.
- Dwarf varieties of sunflower grow to just 12 in (45 cm) and are ideal for pots.
- The sunflower is native to North America, but is the national flower of Russia.
- Sunflower seeds are rich in oil and are full of calcium, iron, and lots of important minerals.

Sowing indoors

Sunflower seeds and yogurt cups

Watering can

Soft string and compost

Larger pot and bamboo stake

1

Plant some seeds into empty yogurt cups using seed compost. Sow a single seed in each, 1 in (3 cm) deep. Water.

2

Put in a sunny place and cover with polyethylene (plastic bag). Soon a shoot will appear; remove the polyethylene.

3

When it outgrows the original container, put it into a bigger pot (with a drainage hole in the bottom) in a sunny spot outdoors when there is no risk of frost.

4

Once your sunflower has started to fade, pick out a few old blossoms and make your very own "sunflower smile."

It's easy to get poked in the eye by the support, so remember to cover the end with something!

TOP HEAVY
Prevent your sunflower from toppling over by securing stems with garden twine to a stout cane or plant stake.

Sowing outdoors

Prepare the soil well by digging over the area and raking it until it resembles fine breadcrumbs. Then sow your seeds 2 in (5 cm) deep, 12 in (45 cm) apart. Cover and water. Three weeks later they should start sprouting.

A food feast

Sunflowers provide nectar for bugs and then a feast of delicious seeds. Once the sunflower has flowered, leave the head to droop and dry and watch as birds, squirrels, and small mammals visit and munch away. Yum! Yum!

This tit picks off the old blossoms with its beak to get to the juicy seeds.

A mini nature reserve

You don't need a big garden to attract wildlife. Plant a window box or even an empty ice cream container and watch the little creatures pay a visit!

What you will need:

Window box

Broken pot and gravel

Compost

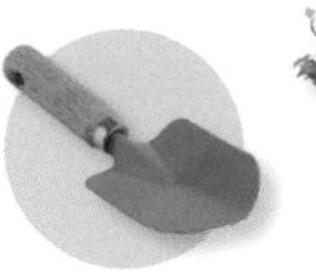
Trowel

Plants–herbs, trailing plants

Saucer or jar lid

1

Make sure the window box has holes in the bottom. Cover the holes with stones.

2

Fill your window box with compost. Then plan out where you'll be positioning the plants.

3

Plant the herbs and trailing plants. Water them well.

4

Mulch the top with gravel or bark to prevent water loss. Add a pinecone as a home for visiting bugs.

For a year-round nature reserve

Plant some flowers, bulbs, and small shrubs that will attract the bugs throughout the year. Here are some suggestions:

Spring

Scented daffodils

Crocuses

Summer

Lavender

Fuchsia

Fall

Pansies

Chrysanthemum

Winter

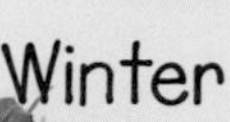

Ivy

Hardy ferns

Chives

EXPERIMENT WITH YOUR MINI RESERVE
Try a herb garden, a meadow patch, or use low-growing woodland plants (in a shady spot).

BE A NATURE DETECTIVE
Note down the names and draw pictures of all the different creatures you attract to your mini reserve.

GO NATIVE
Choose plenty of native plants since these attract most species.

WATER OF LIFE
Include a shallow saucer of water and keep it filled. Wildlife can use it to drink or wash. Also, see if you attract any water bugs.

How to help

Ladybugs and other insects use sheltered places, like window boxes, to hibernate.

Watch it

Keep a nature diary

Keeping a nature diary is a great way to record the changes that go on in your garden throughout the different seasons. It is also a true record of how much different wildlife visits your garden—thanks to all your wildlife gardening efforts! All you need are a few props and some first-rate detective skills.

MY NATURE DIARY

Date → June 18

Today's weather → sunny

Position in garden → by the bird table

Get equipped

You don't need much equipment to be a nature detective:

A notebook is essential to record what you have seen and where you saw it. Fill it up with sketches or photos. Label your pictures.

Binoculars are useful for watching creatures from a distance.

A magnifying glass is handy for a close-up look at small insects.

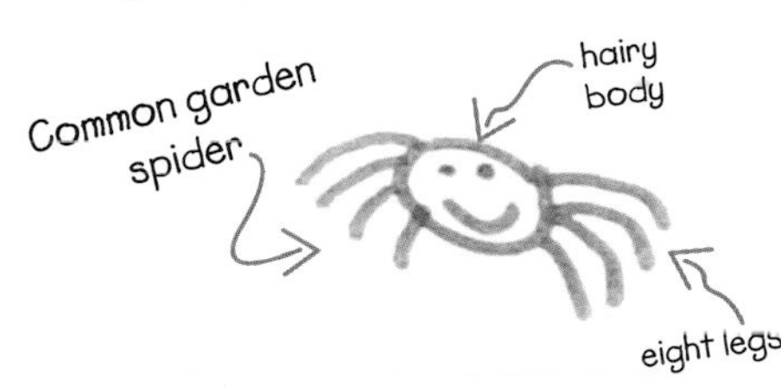

four spots
Ladybug
Ant
head
abdomen
thorax

Where and when to look

You are more likely to see a large variety of creatures between spring and fall, since many animals migrate or hibernate in winter (do not disturb them then). Birds, butterflies, and bees are easy to spot in the open, but some creatures prefer dark, damp places. Worms, ants, centipedes, and millipedes live in soil, while toads, frogs, newts, beetles, and many other insects can be found under fallen leaves, stones, or rotting logs.

tweet!
tweet!

Tell-tale signs

If you are lucky, you can find a lot of creatures very easily, but sometimes they may prove more elusive. Learn to look for footprints in soil—they might belong to a badger or a fox—a feather that has been left behind by a shy bird, or an empty hazelnut that has been eaten by a vole. Some wildlife experts can even tell what animals have been in the garden by the droppings they leave behind.

Animals and activities

Help and encourage wildlife into a new home—your garden—by trying out these activities. All these projects can be done in only a small space, or you could section off part of a garden as your wildlife gardening area. Whatever you choose to do will be greatly appreciated by your new animal neighbors!

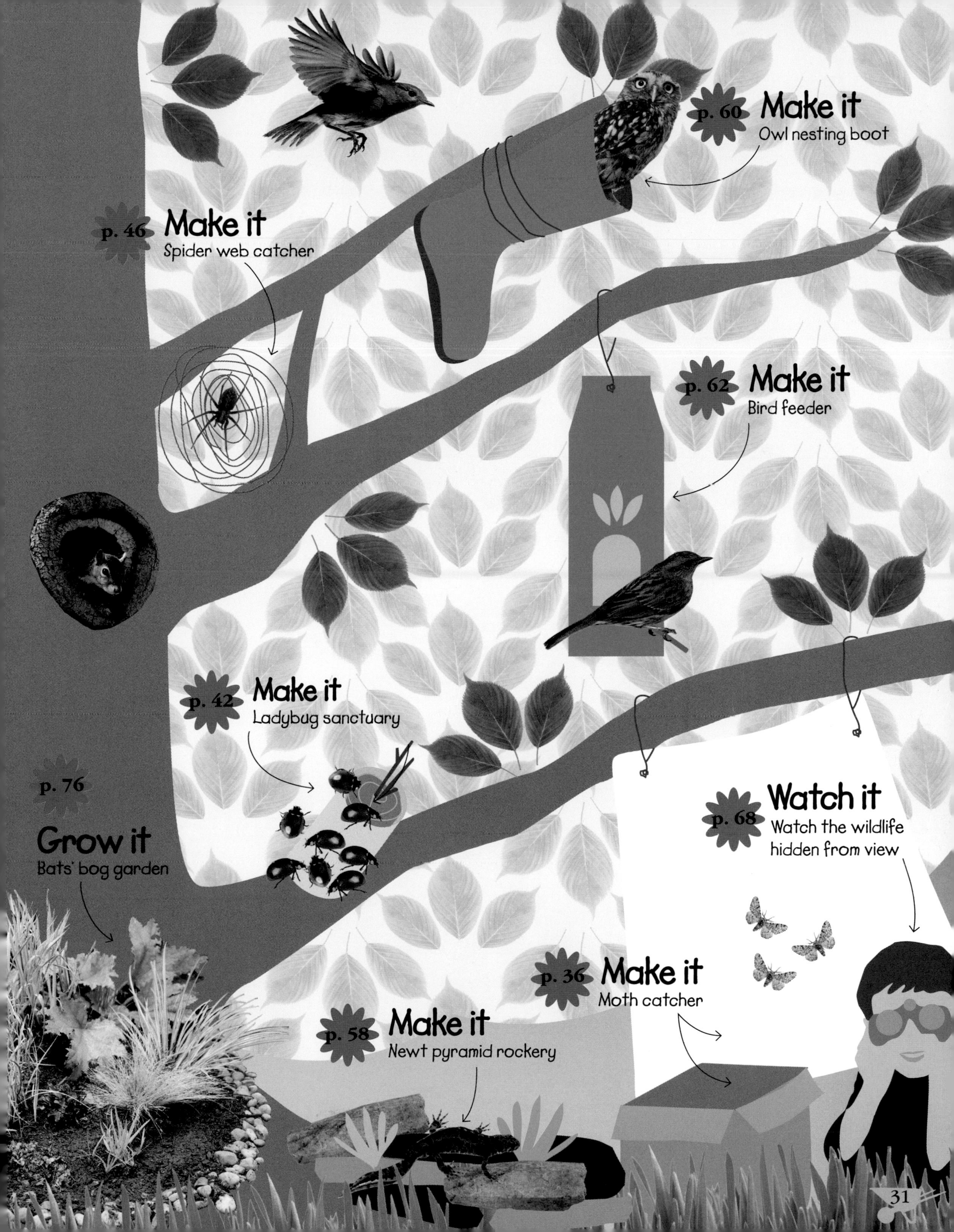

p. 60
Make it
Owl nesting boot
p. 46
Make it
Spider web catcher
p. 62
Make it
Bird feeder
p. 42
Make it
Ladybug sanctuary
p. 76
Grow it
Bats' bog garden
p. 68
Watch it
Watch the wildlife hidden from view
p. 36
Make it
Moth catcher
p. 58
Make it
Newt pyramid rockery

Top 10 Plants for caterpillars and butterflies

Caterpillars are fussy eaters so butterflies have to choose where they lay their eggs carefully. They only choose plants that their hungry offspring are going to eat. Once the caterpillars transform into butterflies, they often seek out a different type of plant altogether—one with nectar-filled flowers.

Plants for caterpillars

1

Nettles (Urtica dioica)

We consider them weeds, but a patch of nettles is the favorite plant for red admiral, peacock, and small tortoiseshell butterflies to lay their eggs. Keep the nettles in a pot to prevent them from spreading.

Sunny or lightly shaded location
Moist soil
Grows 5 ft (1.5 m) high

2

Bird's foot trefoil

(Lotus corniculatus)

Also known as cat's clover, this pretty yellow wild flower with red tips is loved by the caterpillars of many types of butterfly.

Sunny location
Well drained soil
Grows 11 in (30 cm) high

3

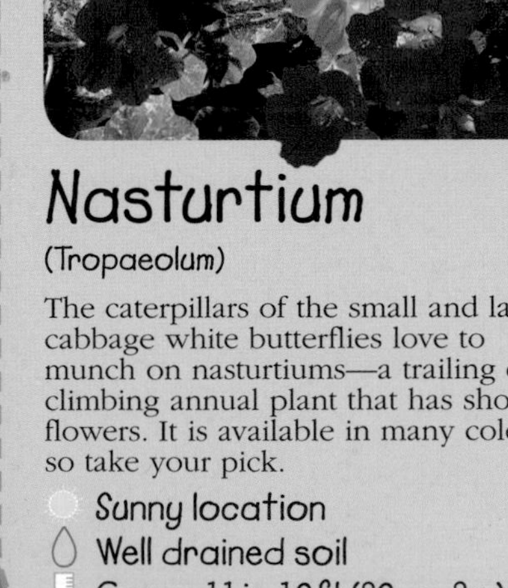

Nasturtium

(Tropaeolum)

The caterpillars of the small and large cabbage white butterflies love to munch on nasturtiums—a trailing or climbing annual plant that has showy flowers. It is available in many colors, so take your pick.

Sunny location
Well drained soil
Grows 11 in–10 ft (30 cm–3 m) high

4

Garlic mustard

(Alliaria petiolata)

Green-veined white butterflies and orange tip butterflies lay eggs on this easy-to-grow plant. Its leaves smell of garlic, and it grows simple white flowers in its second year.

Sunny or partly shaded location
Wet soil
Grows 40 in (1 m) high

Plants for butterflies

5

French marigold

(Tagetes patula)

This small, pretty flower can be found in shades of yellow, orange, and red. The varieties with simple, single flowers are best, but butterflies will visit the double flower marigolds, too.

- Sunny location
- Well drained soil
- Grows 11 in (30 cm) high

6

Helen's flower

(Helenium)

The flowers bloom from late summer into early fall, when masses of daisies smother its upright branches. It spreads slowly but eventually forms into a pretty, flowery clump.

- Sunny location
- Moist soil
- Grows 3 ft (90 cm) high

7

Ice plant

(Sedum spectabile)

The tiny flowers that perch on top of the stems of this plant look like plates—and that's what they are to butterflies—plates of food!

- Sunny location
- Well drained soil
- Grows 18 in (45 cm) high

8

Michaelmas daisy

(Aster novae-belgii)

This is more a bush than a flower and gets covered with daisylike flowers from late summer to fall. There are plenty of flower colors to choose from—all the colors of the rainbow.

- Sunny or partly shaded location
- Moist soil
- Grows 23 in–5 ft (60 cm–1.5 m) high

9

Bugbane

(Cimicifuga simplex)

Bugbane is another great nectar-provider, especially in the fall when butterflies are running out of summer flowers. It has attractive spikes of white flowers.

- Sunny or partly shaded location
- Moist soil
- Grows 4 ft (1.2 m) high

10

Hyssop

(Hyssopus officinalis)

This evergreen herb has a delicious scent and edible leaves. Its spikes of blue flowers last throughout the summer months and into early fall, providing a summer feast for butterflies.

- Sunny location
- Well drained soil
- Grows 23 in (60 cm) high

Make it

Butterfly house

Flitting gracefully from flower to flower to sip sweet nectar, butterflies are delightful to watch. This snug house will give these delicate insects somewhere warm and dry to shelter during bad weather and somewhere safe to hide from predators. The house will also be used by hibernating butterflies over winter and as a resting place at night.

What you will need:

Carton, washed

Scissors

Bark

Glue

Twigs, leaves, and shells

Twine or flexible twig

Did you know?

- Antarctica is the only continent where butterflies have never been found.
- Spot the difference between butterflies and moths when they are still: butterflies generally keep their wings held closely together, while moths keep their wings open flat.

1

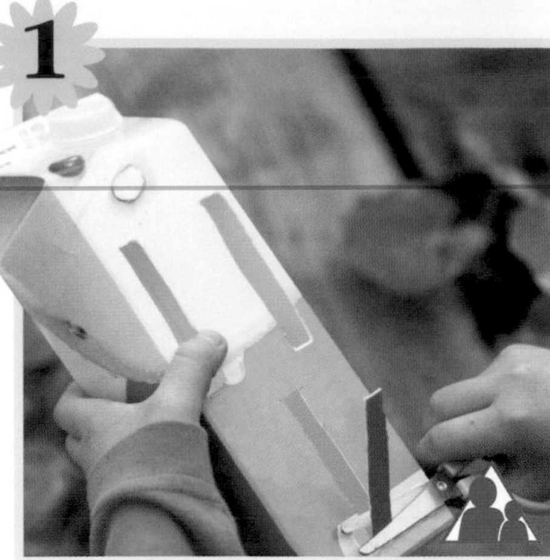

Draw three narrow slits with each one about 2 in (5 cm) long and ½ in (1 cm) wide. Cut them out with scissors.

2

Make a viewing door on another side of the carton. Place a strip of bark inside to provide a place for butterflies to perch.

3

Decorate the carton by sticking on some twigs, leaves, and shells to mimic the natural resting places butterflies seek out.

Butterflies at rest

Trees, grasses, or on the shoots of ivy or other climbing plants are among butterflies' favorite spots to roost. Over winter, some of our best-known butterflies hibernate as adults in the corner of a garage or under a shrub, while others over winter as eggs, and some hibernate as caterpillars in grass stems.

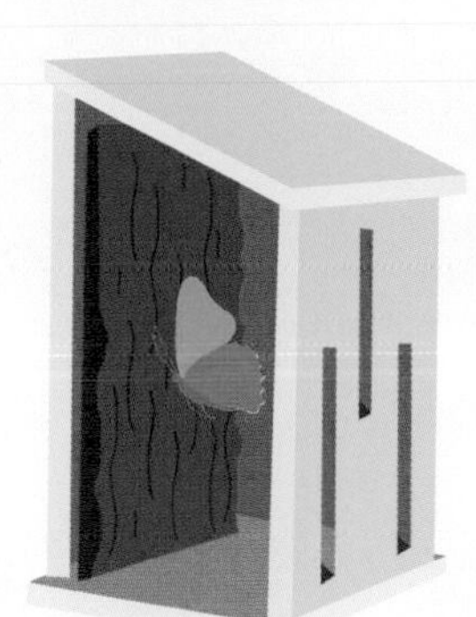

Life cycle

After mating, female butterflies lay their eggs either one by one or in clusters.

These hatch into hungry caterpillars, which will continue to eat until fully grown.

The caterpillar finds somewhere suitable to pupate—often attaching itself head upward to a shoot.

After several weeks, the butterfly emerges from the chrysalis, or pupa.

Make it

Moth catcher

Garden tiger moth

Get a close-up look at moths with this moth catcher. These interesting and beautiful flying insects of the night play a vital role in the food chain—and there's no need to be scared of them.

What you will need:

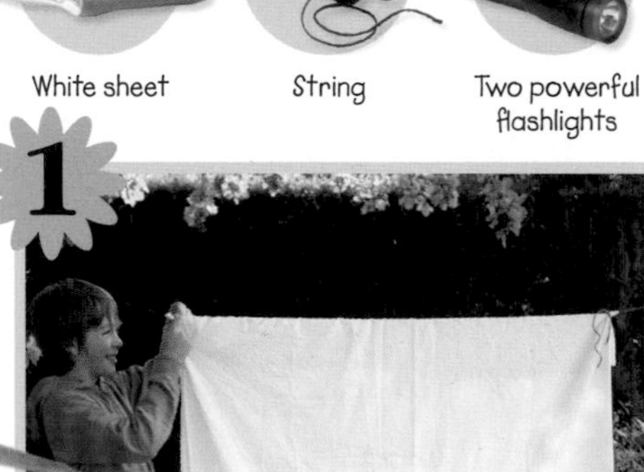
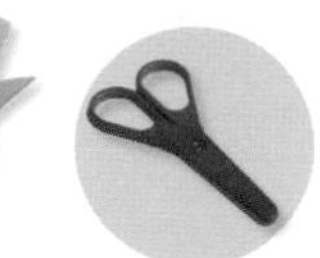

White sheet | String | Two powerful flashlights | Cardboard box | Scissors | Egg cartons, without lids

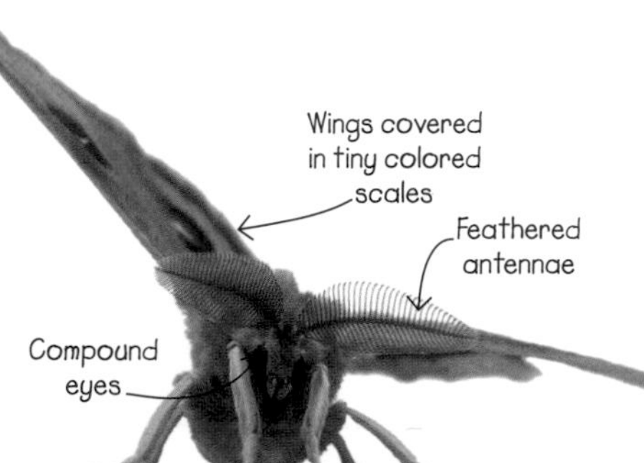

Did you know?

- Moths are masters of disguise. Some are easily mistaken for butterflies since they are so brightly colored, while others look like bees and wasps.
- The life cycle of moths is the same as butterflies.
- There are about 160,000 different moths in the world–many more than the 17,500 butterfly species.
- Many moths actually fly during the daytime.
- Moths are attracted to strongly scented plants after dark and are important pollinators of night-blooming flowers.
- Moths warm up before flying by fluttering their wings.

1

Hang a white sheet between the branches of a tree and use the string to secure in place. (Or, drape a sheet over a wall or a fence instead.)

2

Hang a flashlight behind the sheet or place a powerful flashlight a little distance away in front, pointing at the sheet.

4

Tape four egg cartons inside the box at each end. Scatter the other egg cartons onto the base. The moths will perch on these.

5

Staple the strips to the top of the box so the two remaining flaps make a valley with a narrow slit just over 1 in (3 cm) wide.

Have you ever wondered . . .

why moths are attracted to light? Well, so have scientists but even they are unsure. One theory is that moths confuse lights with the Moon, which they use as a tool to navigate in the dark.

Double-sided tape

Stapler

3

Open all the flaps of the box. Cut off the top flaps on the shortest sides. Then cut one flap into four narrow strips.

6

After dark, switch on both flashlights. Place the box below the sheet and stand the loose flashlight on end inside the box.

Leave the catcher for 1-2 hours. Moths will be drawn to the light shining on the sheet and inside the box. Then, go and take a look!

Afterward, let them go!

Counting moths

Moths are a popular food of many predators, such as birds, toads, lizards, and bats. Scientists use the number of moths as an indicator of the healthiness of the food chain.

TOP 10 Plants for bees

Bees are the ultimate pollen and nectar collectors! They prefer to visit simple, single flowers to complex blooms. So plant some of these top ten plants for bees and soon your garden will be buzzing with life. (Warning! Some bees can give a nasty sting when they feel threatened).

1

Thyme

(Thymus citriodorus)

This herb is an evergreen and spreads to make a mat of gorgeous-smelling foliage. Throughout the summer, the herb is covered with tiny pink flowers that are a great favorite with bees.

- Sunny location
- Well drained soil
- Grows 12 in (30 cm) high

2

Heathers

(Calluna and Erica)

Heathers are small bushes that grow extremely well in acidic soils. They come in many different shapes, sizes, and colors. Some flower in winter, so make sure you choose summer flowering varieties to feed the bees.

- Sunny location
- Acidic, well drained soil
- Grows 12 in (30 cm) high

3

Purple sage

(Salvia officinalis 'Purpurascens')

Another lovely evergreen herb, purple sage has pretty purple leaves that are edible and smell delicious. Bees love the bluish flowers that appear at the tips of the branches in summer.

- Sunny location
- Well drained, moist soil
- Grows 30 in (80 cm) high

6

Verbena

Verbena bonariensis

Verberna has a long wiry stem with a purple pom-pom of flowers at the end. It flowers over a long period, from late spring to the first frosts.

- Sunny location
- Well drained, moist soil
- Grows 60 in (150 cm) high

7

Meadow cranesbill

(Geranium pratense)

Meadow cranesbill has large saucer-shaped purplish flowers that sit above mounds of foliage in early summer. What a beauty!

- Sunny or partly shaded location
- Well drained, moist soil
- Grows 23 in (60 cm) high

8

English lavender

(Lavandula angustifolia)

With its silvery, evergreen leaves and gorgeous scented spikes of purple flowers, lavender bushes are always abuzz with nectar drinkers. In hot weather, lavender smells very strong when it releases its essential oil.

- Sunny location
- Well drained, moist soil
- Grows 40 in (1 m) high

4

Sunflowers

(Helianthus annuus)

Everyone recognizes this old favorite. It has sunny yellow flowers that follow the Sun as it moves across the sky. Bees love its luscious nectar while it is flowering, and birds love to peck out the seeds later in the season.

- Sunny location
- Well drained, moist soil
- Grows 8 ft (2.5 m) high

5

Honeysuckle

(Lonicera varieties)

There are lots of different types and colors of honeysuckle, ranging from white to bright red and some are sweetly scented. This climber is fantastic for covering an empty wall and for feeding the bees in summer.

- Sunny or partly shaded location
- Well drained, moist soil
- Grows 22 ft (7 m) high

9

Hollyhocks

(Alcea rosea)

Almost as tall as a sunflower, a hollyhock really shoots up! Its stems are studded with lots of large flowers that appear from early to mid-summer. They look gorgeous lined up along a wall or fence.

- Sunny location
- Well drained soil
- Grows 5–8 ft (1.5–2.5 m) high

10

Borage

(Borago officinalis)

This will spread quickly around the garden. It has clumps of bristly leaves and bright blue flowers all summer long. You can enjoy these flowers too by floating them on the surface of an ice-cold drink.

- Sunny or partly shaded location
- Well drained soil
- Grows 23 in (60 cm) high

English lavender

Make it

Bee hotel

Buzzing bees make the garden a lively place from spring to fall, busily pollinating many of our favorite plants and food crops. Bees can be attracted by planting lots of nectar- and pollen-rich flowers and providing nesting sites.

What you will need:

½ in (1 cm) diameter
6 in (15 cm) long

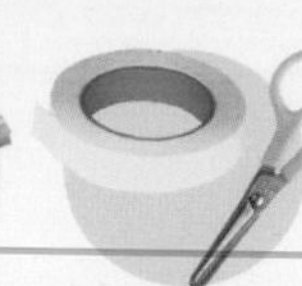

About 20 pieces of bamboo cane

Scissors and strong tape

Modeling clay

Clay pot

Bumble bee

Honey bee

What bee did I see?

There are about 40,000 different species of bee in the world. Nearly 4,000 species of bee are native to the US. Most of them are solitary bees, but there are 45 different bumble bees and one species of honey bee (which is not native).

Did you know?

- Fossils show that bees first appeared on earth 150 million years ago.
- Bees can fly up to speeds of 20 miles (32 km) per hour.
- Unlike honey bees, bumble bees don't die after they have used their sting.

Life cycle

After solitary bees have mated in early spring, the male will die and the female will find a suitable nesting site to lay her eggs.

A mixture of pollen and nectar is placed in each hole in the nest and single eggs laid on these food stores.

When complete, the female seals the holes and nest entrance with mud or chewed-up leaves.

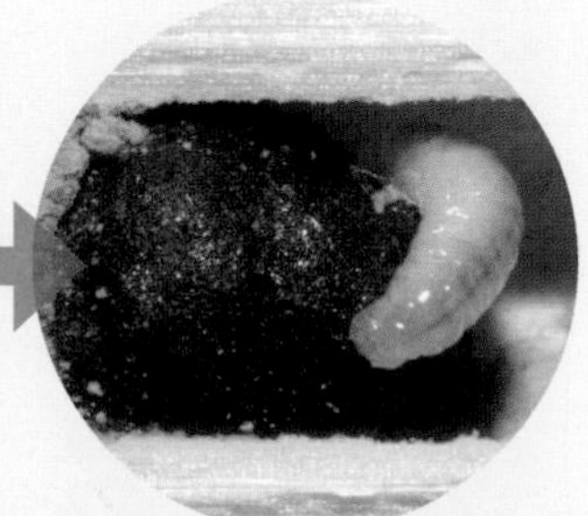

Each newly hatched larva feeds on the stored food. It pupates and emerges as an adult bee next year.

1

Stand the pieces of cane (or hollow plant stems) to make a bundle. Then bind them together, using the tape.

2

Press the canes into a lump of modeling clay to seal off one end.

Put the canes into the pot with the open ends facing outward. Use some more modeling clay to wedge the bundle tightly inside the pot.

4

Leave the pot, with the bottom higher than the opening, in a sunny, dry spot for solitary bees to find.

How to help

Bees are in decline, but the hollow stems of the bamboo canes in this bee hotel will give solitary species somewhere for their young to grow.

Bees in trouble

Sadly, the population of bees is in decline and several species have become extinct over recent years. Loss of habitat, pests, a virus, and even colony collapse disorder (a mysterious ailment of honey bees) have led to their decline. The lower numbers mean fewer pollinators and this has affected the production of flowers and crops.

Other bee hotels

Some solitary bees seek out hollow stems of plants or holes and cracks in bricks, stone walls, or wood to use as nests. As alternative bee hotels, ask an adult to drill a series of 6 in (15 cm) deep holes, with ¼ in (6-10 mm) diameter, into a piece of untreated wood or pile up some bricks with holes facing outward.

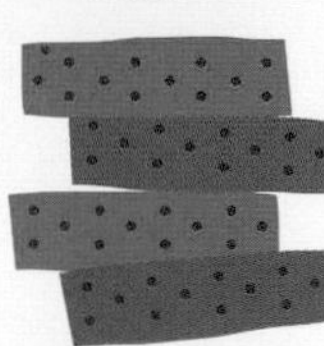

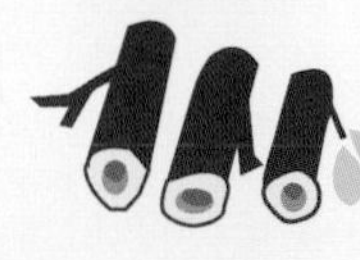

Make it

Ladybug sanctuary

Ladybugs are a gardener's best friend. Although tiny, these instantly recognizable spotted creatures have a ravenous appetite for aphids and other tiny pests that cause damage to plants. Welcome them into your garden by providing a shelter.

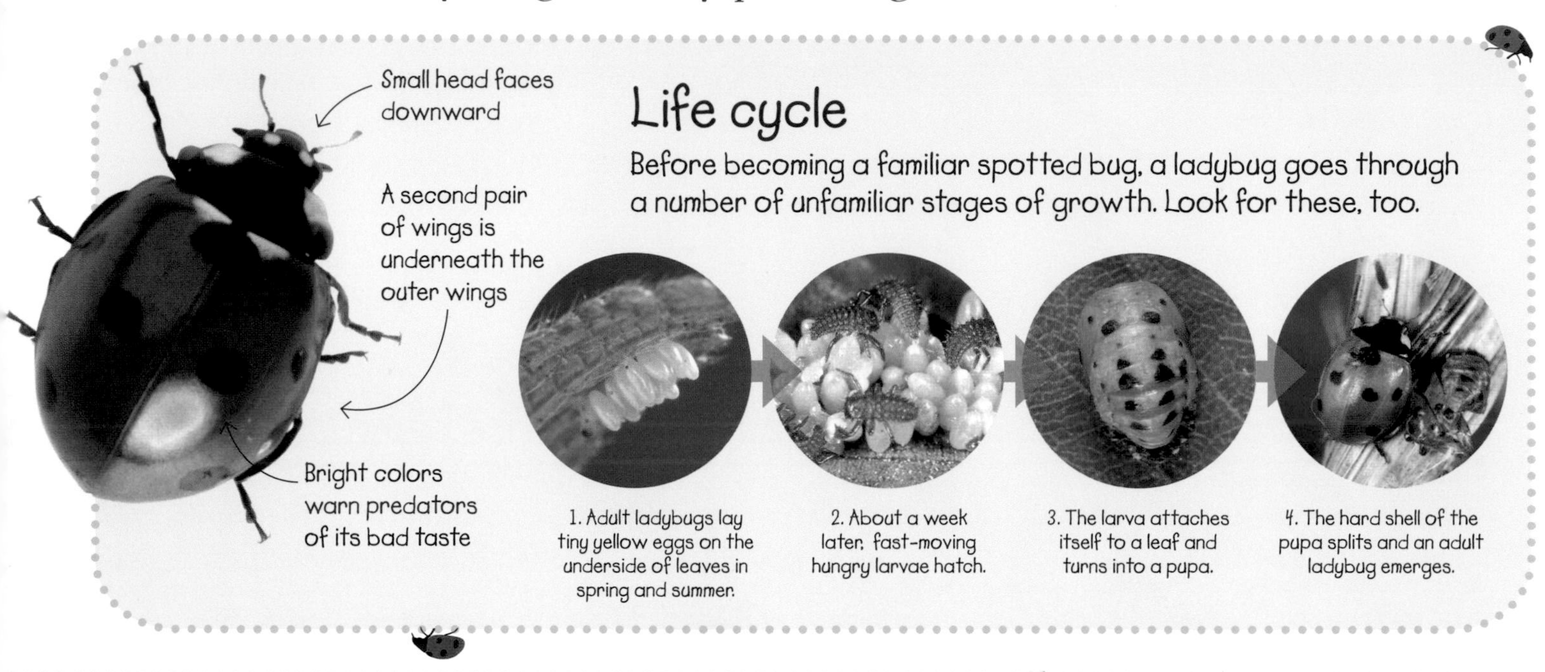

Life cycle

Before becoming a familiar spotted bug, a ladybug goes through a number of unfamiliar stages of growth. Look for these, too.

1. Adult ladybugs lay tiny yellow eggs on the underside of leaves in spring and summer.
2. About a week later, fast-moving hungry larvae hatch.
3. The larva attaches itself to a leaf and turns into a pupa.
4. The hard shell of the pupa splits and an adult ladybug emerges.

What you will need:

¼ in (6 mm) tubes

Corrugated cardboard

Scissors

Plastic bottle, washed

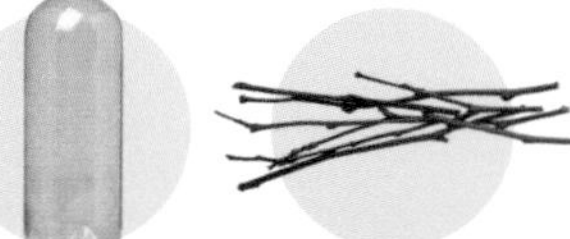

Twigs

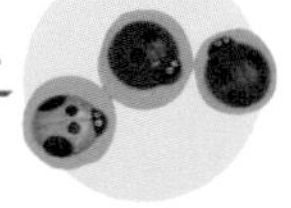

Decorations (optional)

1

Ask an adult to cut the top off a plastic bottle. Cut out a piece of the corrugated cardboard about the length of the bottle, remembering to cut across the tubes.

2

Roll the corrugated cardboard up as tightly as possible without crushing the tubes too much. Place the rolled-up cardboard into the plastic bottle and stack up the sides.

3

Fill the hole with twigs for the ladybugs to land on. Place the bottle in a dry, sheltered spot. Among conifers or shrubs are good places.

How to help

Ladybugs need to hibernate over winter. This sanctuary will keep them snug, warm, and dry until they are ready to emerge in the spring.

4

The bottom of the bottle needs to be higher than the opening to allow water to drain away.

Hibernation

Ladybugs often use the same site to hibernate every year and sometimes hibernate together in large colonies that number in the hundreds. It is thought that they release a scent to attract others since huddling together to keep warm improves their chances of surviving the winter.

A single ladybug can eat up to 5,000 aphids in its lifetime.

Did you know?

- There are a staggering 5,000 different ladybugs worldwide.
- Ladybug species vary in color, size, and number of spots around the world.
- If frightened, ladybugs release a strong smelling yellow goo to warn off predators.

Make it

Stag beetle bucket

The male stag beetle is a spectacular creature, with its large antlers or jaws at the front of its body. Two-thirds of the 30 species in the US live in the western part of the country, preferring light, well drained soil. In some places, the removal of the stag beetle's natural habitat, including dead tree stumps, means it is now rarely seen. Here's an idea to help it and other beetles survive.

What you will need:

Plastic bucket

Craft knife

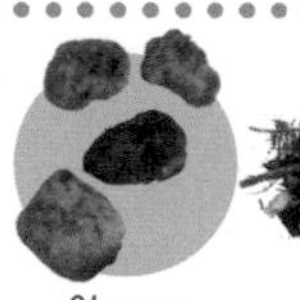
Stones

Wood chips

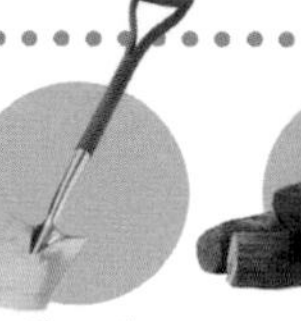
Shovel

Logs

1

Ask an adult to make holes about 1 in (3 cm) across in the sides and base of the plastic bucket using a craft knife. The female stag beetle will crawl through these holes to lay her eggs.

2

Choose an area of your garden that will not be disturbed for at least five years—the length of a stag beetle's life cycle. Dig a hole deep enough to bury the bucket so that its rim is just below soil level.

3

Loosely fill any gaps around the bucket with soil. Place a few large stones in the bottom to slow the draining of the rainwater. Then place 1 or 2 logs—oak is best—upright in the bucket.

Did you know?

- Female stag beetles do not have the distinctive large antlers and can release a perfume to attract males.
- Adult stag beetles can be seen flying at dusk in summer.
- Male stag beetles sometimes wrestle other males to win a female.
- They have many enemies that eat them, including cats, magpies, crows, and foxes.

The wing case protects the wings underneath

These two males are using their antlers to fight.

Life cycle

Adult stag beetles emerge and mate in early summer. The female lays her eggs in the stumps and roots of dead deciduous trees and dies shortly afterward. Cream colored grubs with brown heads feed on the decaying wood for up to five years before pupating. When fully grown, the C-shaped larvae are about 3 in (8 cm) long.

This life-size one year old stag beetle larva is munching its way through the rotten wood.

5

Mark the area with a pile of logs for other beetles to use. Leave the area undisturbed.

4

Fill the bucket with wood chips and add a little potting soil. The female stag beetle will lay her eggs on the logs and the larvae will feed on the wood as it rots.

How to help

Stag beetles lay eggs on dead wood in the soil so that the larvae will have food after hatching. This bucket mimics these conditions.

Make it

Spider web catcher

Spiders are fascinating creatures that are a delight to watch, especially when they are spinning an intricate web. Get up close using this web catcher. Although some people fear them, spiders help by catching many plant-eating insects.

Did you know?

- Spiders are not insects but belong to a group known as arachnids.
- Most spiders live for about a year, but tarantulas have been known to live as long as 15 years or more.
- There are at least 30,000 species of spider in the world.
- Some spiders' bodies measure just 0.03 in (1 mm) in length, while tarantulas are a whopping 3½ in (90 mm).
- The majority of spiders have four pairs of eyes—two on the front and two on top of the head.
- Circular webs are most familiar, but some spiders spin funnel or bowl-shaped webs.

Each leg has seven segments

Bristles on the legs pick up the senses

Fangs for injecting venom into prey

Life cycle

After mating, female spiders find a safe place to lay their eggs. These hatch into spiderlings—tiny, perfect replicas of the adult spider. Some will remain active all year round, while others will hibernate over winter, or die after laying their eggs.

What you will need:

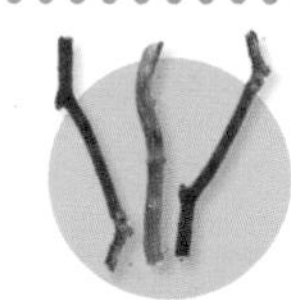

3 medium-long, straightish sticks.

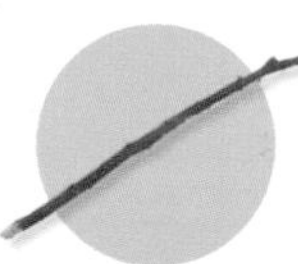

1 longer thicker stick

Four lengths of garden twine

1

Make a triangular shape with sides about 10 in (25 cm), using the twine to tie the sticks together at the corners.

2

Attach the large stick about 3 ft (1 m) long, to the triangle, using the last piece of twine. You now have your web catcher.

3

In late summer, push the long stick into the ground, near a place you have seen spiders. Check each morning. Be patient.

Different types

All spiders can produce silk, but not all spin webs to help trap their prey. Some hide in burrows and ambush an unwary insect, while others actively hunt and chase their next meal.

Trapdoor spiders lie in wait just below the opening to their burrows ready to pounce if they sense movement.

Packed lunch

A spider injects a venom into its prey and wraps it up in silk. The venom turns the prey's insides into a liquid, which the spider drinks.

Hey presto! A glistening web inside the catcher.

Make it

Wormery

Wriggly, slippery, and slimy earthworms are mysterious soil-dwelling creatures. With this wormery, you can watch them at work, stirring up the soil layers underground.

Did you know?

- There are 3,000 different worms in the world.
- Common earthworms can measure up to 13 in (35 cm) long, which is a fraction of the size of a tropical species that grows to more than 40 in (1 m).
- Birds, foxes, toads, badgers, shrews, and many other creatures eat worms as part of their diet.
- A worm's burrow can be as deep as 60 in (150 cm).

Earthworms have no eyes, ears, or noses but can sense light and vibrations.

What you will need:

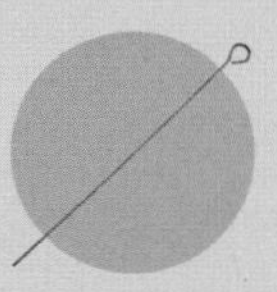

Clear jar, washed

Skewer

Sand

Strips of newspaper, moist

Leaf litter, large handful

A little compost

1

Poke some holes into the bottom and near the top of the jar, using the skewer. Pour sand in to make a 4 in (10 cm) layer.

2

Add the moist newspaper strips. Pour in the leaves and a little compost and soil for the worms' bedding. Add more sand.

3

Collect some worms by digging up some soil or spraying the soil and covering with a plastic bag for an hour. Put them in the jar.

Types of worms

Worms are invertebrates—creatures without any bones. There are two main types: earthworms that live in the soil and composting worms, which are produced on large farms and bred specially for large wormeries.

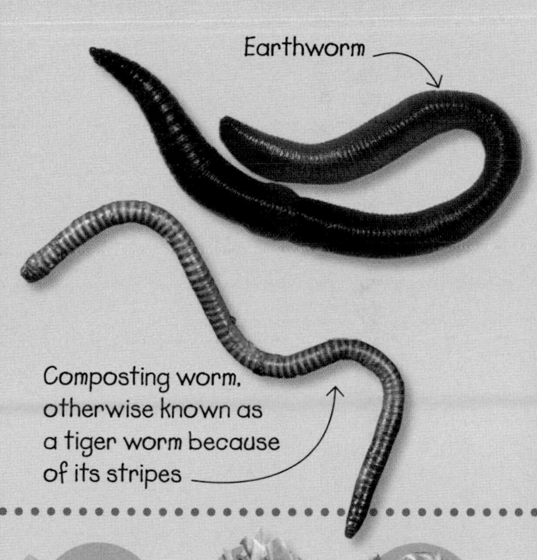

A little soil

Scrap food—fruit and vegetable peelings

Add some food scraps as food for the worms. Cover the jar and place it in a cool, dark place for a couple of weeks.

Composters

Without worms, plants would struggle to grow. At night, worms drag dead leaves or other debris under the soil to eat. After digesting, worms leave coiled casts (poop), which are high in nutrients for the plants on the soil's surface.

Worms in action

The worms' tunneling activity underground helps to aerate the soil and improve its drainage. This also helps plants to grow.

AFTERCARE
Add more food scraps as the worms use up their supply. Empty your wormery onto the soil when you're finished.

Make it

Snail race track

Gardeners may dislike snails for munching their plants but snails are fun to watch, sliding along on a muscular foot. Cheer them on as the snails slime in their irregular winding way across this race track.

What you will need:

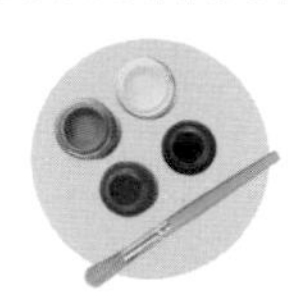
Paint

Cardboard

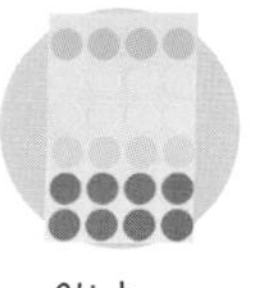
Stickers

Pen

Snails

Watch

1

Draw a series of circles radiating outward onto a piece of cardboard because snails don't move in straight lines.

2

Paint the circles. The center one will be the starting point and the outer ones mark the finish line.

3

Number the snails to identify them. Write numbers onto the stickers and stick one on each snail's shell.

4

Place the snails into the center and let them go. The winning snail is the one that has gone the farthest in five minutes or reached the finish line first.

Life cycle

A land snail starts life as an egg and hatches into a miniature adult. It usually lives between five to ten years.

Eggs are laid in a nest just below the soil surface.

After nine days, the eggs become transparent and tiny snails with shells can be seen inside.

A few weeks later, a hungry newborn snail hatches and sets off in search of food.

Yummy leaf!

Did you know?

- There are about 50,000 different land snails in the world.
- Snails are most active at night and during damp weather.
- The shells grow as the snails get older. Snails produce calcium carbonate, which is added to the opening of the shell to allow the spiral to enlarge.
- When the weather is too dry, a snail retreats into its shell and seals the entrance to form a hard cap.

Watch it

Pond dipping

Ponds are fascinating places to explore for wildlife. In this watery world you will find many unusual and bizarre-looking creatures. Many of them are fierce predators, lurking among the plants ready to pounce on their prey.

Life cycle

Dragonflies make a dramatic transformation during their life cycle. Their lives begin in water and end on land.

A female dragonfly lays eggs in or near the water on aquatic plants.

The eggs hatch as nymphs, which eat huge numbers of other pond creatures.

When a nymph is fully grown after 2–7 years, it climbs to the top of a pond plant and its skin splits.

An adult emerges and dries its wings in the sun before flying off. Most adults live for about two months.

Tadpole

IMPORTANT: Always return the creatures you have caught to the same part of the pond.

What will you find?

Slowly sweep your net through the water. Turn the net inside-out into a container that is half-filled with water. Take a close look and see what you can identify. Here are some animals often found in ponds.

FOR SAFETY, always have an adult with you when near a pond, stream, or river.

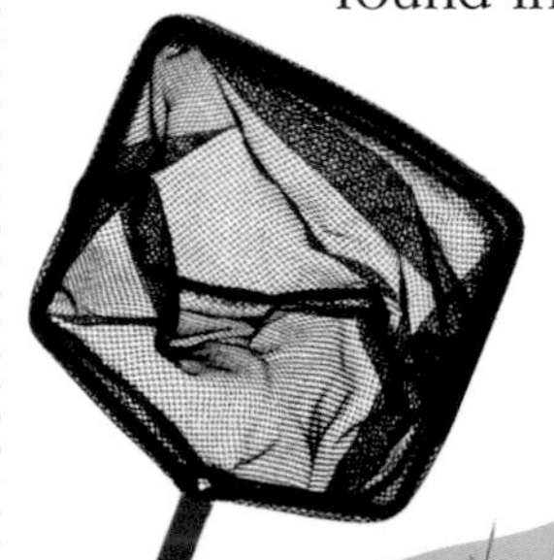

A DIP NET has a fine mesh to trap tiny creatures.

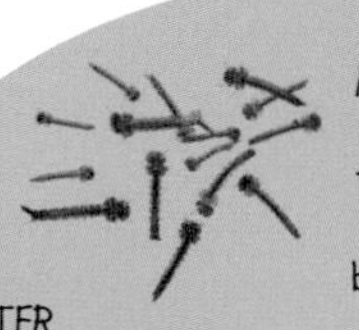

MOSQUITO LARVAE swim just beneath the water or hang upside down just below the surface.

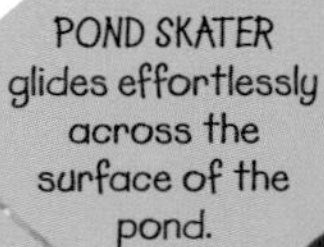

POND SKATER glides effortlessly across the surface of the pond.

WATER BEETLE LARVA is a fierce carnivore. Don't touch—it has powerful jaws and sharp fangs.

GREATER WATERBOATMAN swims upside down near the surface of the pond. Don't touch since it bites.

POND SNAIL looks like its land relative but it eats pond plants and rotting plants.

DAMSELFLY NYMPH has a ravenous appetite and looks fearsome.

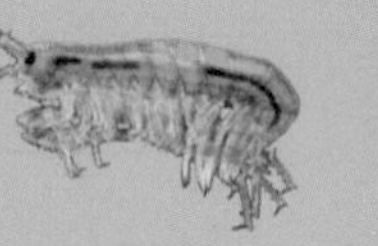

FRESHWATER SHRIMP can be found at the edges of ponds or under stones.

FRESHWATER LEECH is a flattened wormlike creature that is eaten by fish and insect larvae.

ANY LUCK?
Try dipping through an area of weeds since many animals hide away in them.

Water plants

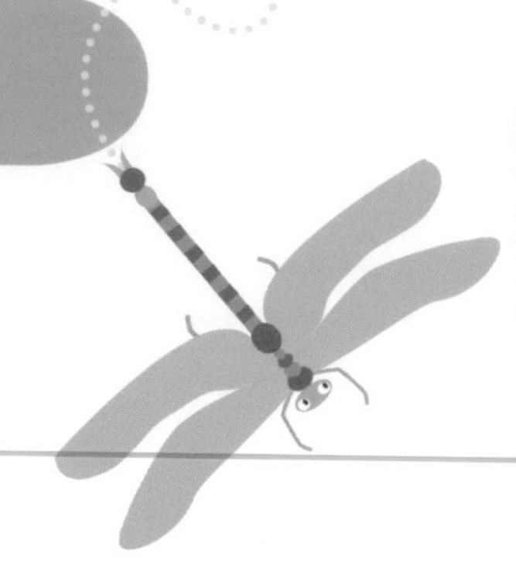

Big or small, your pond will be all the better for some well-chosen pond plants. They will keep the water healthy and clear, and provide hiding places for animals. Here are our top ten.

• **Oxygenating plants** help to keep the water clear.

• **Deep water plants** help to keep the pond cool.

1

Hornwort

(*Ceratophyllum demersum*)

This bristly leaved plant spends most of its life under water, but the stems do float to the surface during summer, where buds eventually break off, sink to the bottom, and take root.

- Sunny or lightly shaded location
- Wet soil
- Needs 35 in (90 cm) water depth

3

Water hawthorn

(*Aponogeton distachyos*)

This attractive plant has purple-tinted leaves and tiny white flowers. It appears above the surface of the water from early spring to fall.

- Sunny or partly shaded location
- Wet soil
- Needs 11–35 in (30–90 cm) water depth

4

Golden club

(*Orontium aquaticum*)

The golden club breaks the surface of the water in the late spring, with a pretty rosette of slender oval leaves.

- Sunny or partly shaded location
- Wet soil
- Needs 17 in (45 cm) water depth

2 Hair grass

(*Eleocharis acicularis*)

Once you have put this on the bottom of your pond you will not see it again, since this carpeting plant, which resembles grass, stays under water all the time.

- Sunny or lightly shaded location
- Wet soil
- Needs 35 in (90 cm) water depth

Bog plants are planted in the wet soil around the pond's edge.

You'll need a mix of the four types of pond plants
- Oxygenating plants
- Deep water plants
- Floating plants
- Marginal plants

Floating plants may have roots hanging free in the water.

• Floating plants provide surface cover and stop the water from turning green.

5 Frog's bit

(Hydrocharis morsus-ranae)

Frog's bit forms a mass of lovely rounded leaves that float on the surface. In summer, it grows thin stalks with beautiful three-petaled flowers at the ends.

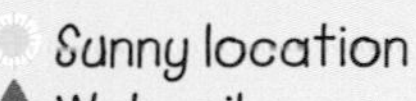

Sunny location
Wet soil
Short floater

6 Water soldier

(Stratiotes aloides)

More suitable for a large pond, the rosette of sword-shaped leaves of the water soldier emerges from the water in summer, followed by pretty white flowers. Dragonflies may use the plant as a perch and eat the bugs the plant attracts.

Sunny location
Wet soil
Short floater

7 Common bladderwort

(Utricularia vulgaris)

This carnivorous plant has tiny air-filled sacks covered with minute hairs on the stems. When a sack is touched by a water bug, the sack opens and water rushes in, along with the creature.

Sunny location
Wet soil
Short floater

• Marginals provide protection to pond creatures.

8 Water forget-me-not

(Myosotis scorpiodes)

This plant has lots of flower power. From late spring until the beginning of summer, its shoots are smothered in heaps of tiny blue flowers.

Sunny or partly shaded location
Wet soil
Grows 17 in (45 cm) high

9 Branched bur-reed

(Sparganium erectum)

This reed has tall, narrow sword-shaped leaves that hide the flowering stems. The white flowers become tiny burred seed heads in the fall.

Sunny or partly shaded location
Wet soil
Grows 40 in (1 m) high

10 Cattails

(Typha minima)

The plant's perky grassy shoots grow like upright spears. The thin flowering spike holds a brown seed head about the size of an acorn.

Sunny or partly shaded location
Wet soil
Grows 24 in (60 cm) high

Make it

Frog and toad home

Spotting a toad or a frog is exciting. They are not only interesting to watch, but they also gobble up many creatures that we consider pests. Make them feel welcome by building them a special home.

How to help

Toads and frogs like a cool and damp shallow burrow to hide away in during the day and to hibernate in over winter.

What you will need:

Trowel

Clay pot

Damp leaves

Watering can

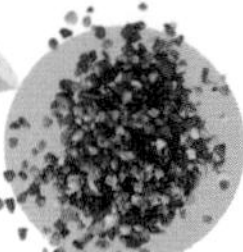
Gravel

Saucer

1

Find a cool, moist place in the shade. Dig out a hole with a trowel, making the hole a bit longer than the clay pot.

2

Place the pot on its side into the hole and bury about half of it, by filling the inside with some soil.

3

Use some damp leaves to make a nice bed for the frog or toad inside the pot.

4

Moisten the area with a little water to keep the pot in place.

Spot the difference

- Frogs have smooth, damp skin, while toads are warty and dry.
- Frogs tend to hop when they move, while toads walk.
- Frogs appear in many colors and can change their shade depending on temperature or mood. The color of toads varies with their habitats. Those living on dark soil are a browner color than those on gray soil.

Toads' diet

Toads have a healthy appetite and have a long list of favorite foods.

5

Place a small saucer nearby with some gravel and a small amount of water in it for the frog or toad to splash around.

Newt pyramid rockery

Newts are rarely seen amphibians that you can attract to the garden by making a pond and building a rockery hideaway for them in a damp spot nearby. Make sure your pond has no fish in it as they eat newt larvae.

What you will need:

Large flat stones

Leaf litter

Soil

Rockery plants

Find a sheltered, south-facing spot with foliage above and around. Place the largest flat stones on the bottom and the smaller stones on top. Leave gaps between them.

Press leaves into the gaps to make a nice bed for the newts and a perfect place to hide away.

Add soil in between some of the stones where the rockery plants will be planted.

Did you know?

- Newts love to eat slugs, worms, and insects and their larvae.
- Newts have lots of predators, including water beetles, dragonfly larvae, and grass snakes.

Newts shed their skin often

Webbing between toes

Tail used as a paddle in water

Female newts lay single eggs on folded leaves.

A larva forms inside the clear egg-case.

Newt larva have feathery gills and live in the water.

After a gradual change, adult newts leave the pond to find hiding places.

Hibernation

After leaving the water in the summer, newts spend a few months on land before hibernating under stones, leaves, and logs for much of the winter.

4

Plant the rockery plants in the soil-filled areas. We used cowslip, houseleek, sedum, and aubrieta.

Conservation

Newts are found in North America, Europe, and Asia. However, the number of newts has fallen due to pollution and to the destruction of their habitats.

HANDLING: Newts might look cute but do not handle them unless they are in danger. If you do pick them up, make sure your hands are wet and be gentle. Wash your hands very well afterward.

Make it

Owl nesting boot

Did you know?

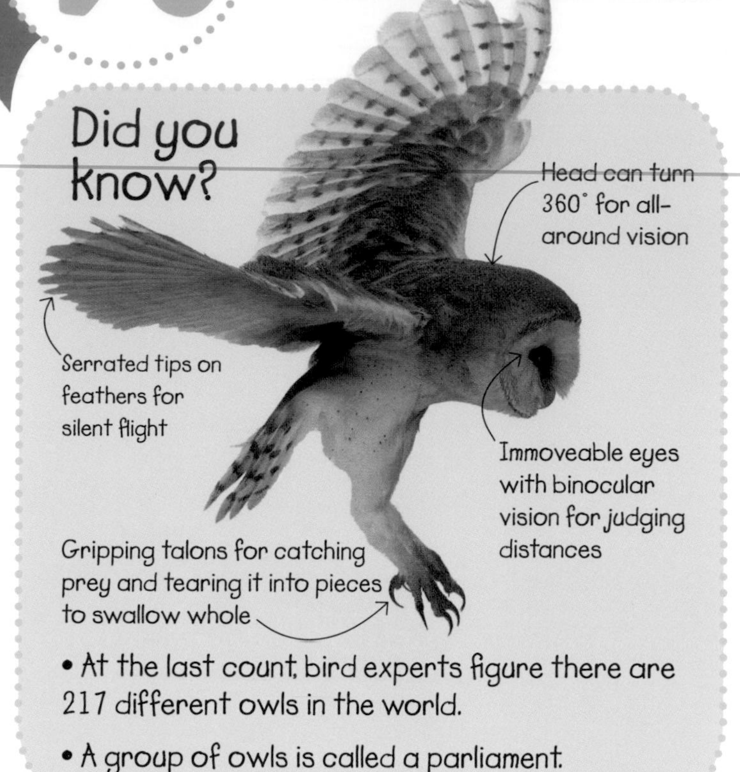

- At the last count, bird experts figure there are 217 different owls in the world.
- A group of owls is called a parliament.

Owls are not common, and mainly come out after dark, but they are amazing birds that you might spot if you're lucky. Improve your chances by giving them somewhere to nest and listen for their distinctive hooting call. Owls are birds of prey and feast on small creatures, such as birds, rodents, and reptiles. If your garden contains places for their prey to live, it may become an owl's favorite hunting ground.

Pygmy owls are just 7 in (17 cm) tall, while the largest eagle owls are 2½ ft (76 cm) tall.

What you will need:

Adult-sized rain boot

Skewer

Wood shavings or sawdust

Stapler

Wire

Ladder

1

Poke several holes in the bottom of the boot with a skewer so that rainwater and other liquid waste can drain out.

2

Drop two handfuls of wood shavings or sawdust into the boot to cover the base as bedding for the eggs and owlets.

3

Secure the boot in place by wrapping the wire around the branch and the boot. Staple the wire to the boot if necessary.

Best position
Attach the boot on a tree 10 ft (3 m) up and along a sturdy branch at a 45° angle to prevent rainwater from getting in.

4

How to help
Many natural nesting sites are under threat. This treetop refuge will give small species of owls somewhere safe and warm to raise their young.

Look for signs of use such as white droppings on the sides of the boot, on the branch, or on the ground below. After the owls have left the nest, clean out the boot and add more sawdust ready for the next family of owls.

Nesting habits

The place where owls make a nest depends on the species. Little owls prefer to lay their three to five white eggs in a narrow hollow in late spring. These will hatch about four weeks later. Owlets leave the nest after three weeks, but are still reliant on their parents for food for some time.

Bird feeder

Watching garden birds is lots of fun and they are among the easiest creatures to attract to your garden. All you need to do is hang up a feeder and fill it with the food that birds love to eat.

What you will need:

Carton, washed

Plastic bags

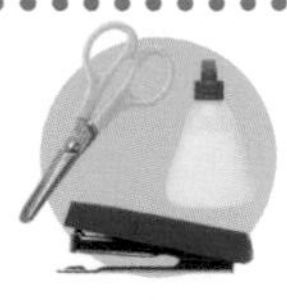

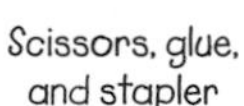

Scissors, glue, and stapler

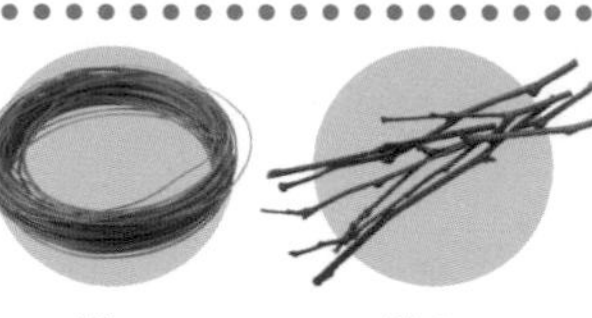

Wire

Twigs

Bird seed, good quality

Did you know?

- In the world, there are about 10,000 different species of birds.
- House sparrows are the most widely spread wild bird around the world, but their numbers have declined dramatically in recent years in some countries.
- House martins have great homing instincts. They breed in Europe, then fly to Africa and Asia for the winter, before flying back to the same nest in spring.
- Many tits have a huge appetite for caterpillars, and adults will gather up to 10,000 caterpillars for their young.

1

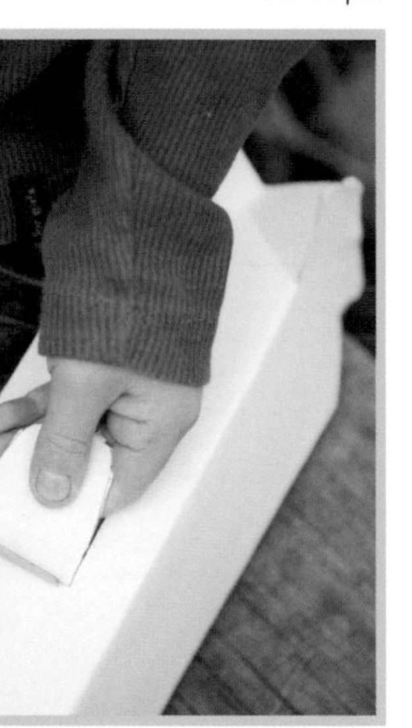

Cut a hole in the side of the clean carton about 2 in (5 cm) from the bottom. This will be the doorway of the feeder.

2

Cut out some brown and green leaf shapes from plastic bags and stick them on the carton with the glue.

3

Poke several small holes in the bottom of the carton with scissors so that water can drain out when it rains.

4

Staple the top opening closed. Pierce another hole in the top and thread the wire through for hanging up the feeder.

5
Poke a twig through the carton just below the doorway for a perch. Add bird seed and hang the feeder.

Other bird feeders

Birds' diet

Birds like different things to eat, such as fruits or bugs, and have different ways of eating, either on the ground or from the safety of trees. In the spring, birds need lots of insects, which are high in protein, to give to their young, while high-fat foods give the birds energy to survive the winter. We can help by putting out peanuts, seeds, apples, and high-fat balls, especially over winter when food is scarce for the birds.

Make it

Bathroom for birds

Many gardeners are in the habit of putting food out for birds, but few remember to give them some water. A birdbath and shower will give them somewhere to drink and to wash, keeping them healthy and happy.

What you will need:

Shallow bowl

Small stones, rinsed

Shells and pebbles, rinsed

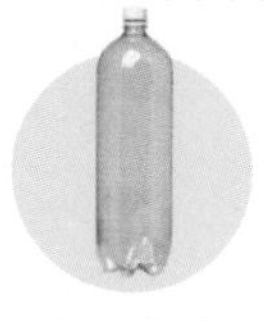
Clean plastic bottle with cap

Push pin and watering can

String

1

Cover the bottom of a shallow bowl with a layer of small stones. Place the bowl on a small sturdy table or a level tree stump.

2

Add a small decoration such as a pebble sculpture, a flagpole, or a plastic frog to your birdbath.

3

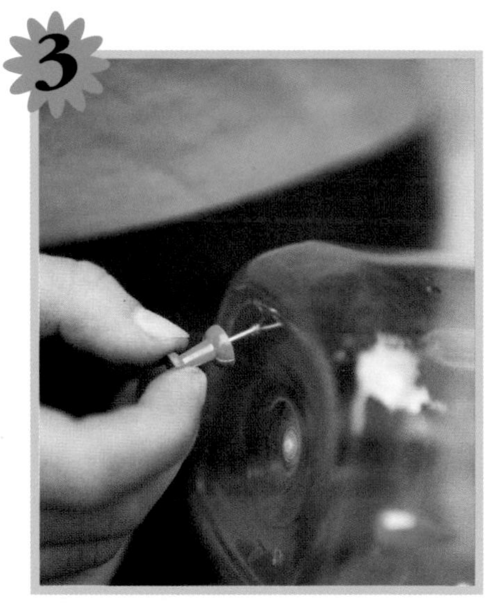

Make a tiny hole in the bottom of the bottle, using the tip of a push pin. Decorate the bottle if you wish.

4

Add water to the bottle and screw on the bottle cap. The water will flow in a stream at first, then slow to a steady drip.

5

Attach the string to the cap of the bottle. Hang the bottle from a branch above the bowl so that the water drips into it. The rippling effect will attract the birds.

6

Add some water to the bowl. Every few weeks, clean the bowl with soapy water to remove droppings and to prevent the buildup of bacteria.

Empty snail shells placed in the bowl will attract the birds to the birdbath.

Did you know?

• Birds drink in different ways. Some scoop up the water in flight, others dip in their beaks and throw back their heads to swallow, and others immerse their bills and drink continuously.

• Birds use water to wash dirt from their feathers, which makes it easier for them to preen—rearrange their feathers and spread oil from a preen gland near their tails over their bodies to keep their feathers waterproof.

Birds use their bills to cover their feathers with the oil.

Seed-eating birds, such as sparrows, need to drink at least twice a day.

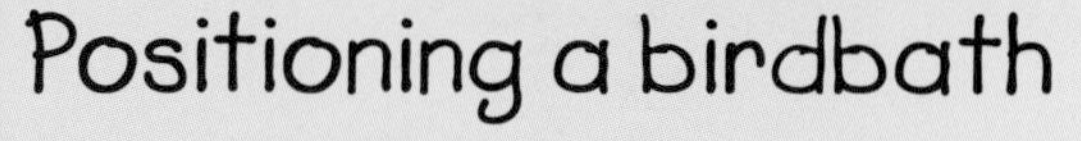

Positioning a birdbath

Refill your birdbath with fresh water whenever supplies are running low.

When birds drink or bathe they are vulnerable to attack from predators, so birds will only visit your birdbath if they feel safe. Place it where they can clearly see the garden and close to bushes, where they can fly to if they become alarmed. Avoid placing it above ground-covering shrubs from where cats could mount an ambush.

Make it

Flower pot birdhouse

Birds need somewhere warm, snug, and safe to lay their eggs and raise their young. They use nooks and crannies in trees and hedges, or hollows in the ground. Putting up nesting boxes is ideal where these sites are scarce.

What you will need:

Plastic flower pot and base

String

Scissors or craft knife

Strong glue

Decorations

Waterproof tape

Thread some string through the holes on the bottom of the pot and tie the ends together for a secure hanging loop.

Cut a 1 in (3 cm) hole in the side of the pot, 2 in (5 cm) from the bottom. Make some small holes in the base for drainage.

Glue around the edge of the base and stick to the bottom of the pot as a base for the birdhouse.

Decorate the birdhouse with dried flowers, shells, twigs, or pinecones, using the glue.

Cover the top with strips of bark stuck down using waterproof tape. The bark will stop rainwater from dripping onto the nest.

A perfect home

Different-sized birds are attracted to different nest boxes, depending on the size of the entrance hole. Some boxes even have several holes in them to attract birds that like to live in large groups. Birds

Parenting skills

Birds look for a suitable nesting site between late winter and early spring before they mate. After the nest is built, the female lays her eggs, then sits on them until they hatch. The parents feed the fledglings until they have learned to fly and are ready to leave the nest.

BEST PLACE
Rest the pot on a strong branch sheltered among some leaf cover. Secure in place by using the hanging loop.

will use all kinds of things to line their nests including hair, sheep wool, moss, twigs, straw, bits of paper, and blades of grass.

Watch it

Hide and seek

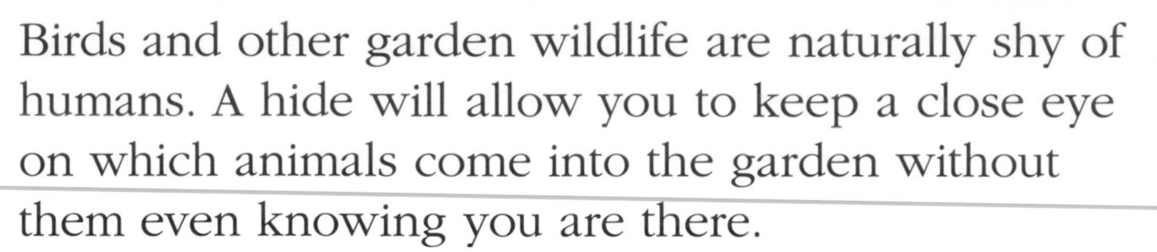

Birds and other garden wildlife are naturally shy of humans. A hide will allow you to keep a close eye on which animals come into the garden without them even knowing you are there.

What you will need:

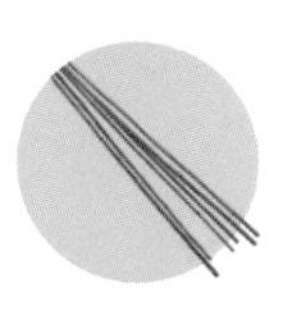
8 stakes

String

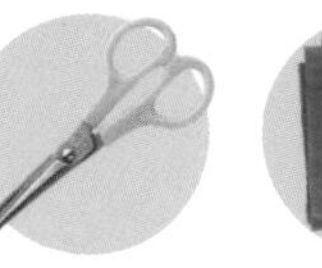
Scissors

Dark green mesh or netting

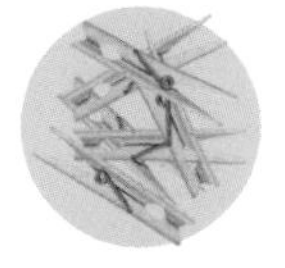
Clothespins

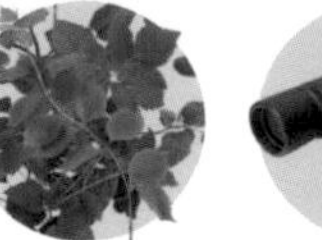
Leafy branches

Binoculars

1

Make the hide structure by tying the stakes together with the string. Make sure the structure doesn't wobble around.

2

Drape the mesh over the top of the stakes. Use the clothespins to attach the mesh to the stakes to stop it from flapping.

3

Poke some leafy branches through the mesh to camouflage the hide. Cut out two peep holes in the mesh at eye level.

Watching wildlife

Wildlife can be cautious and will not stick around for long if they become aware of humans. Noise, scent, and the sight of you will have them heading out of the garden very quickly. Here are five simple ways to keep them from becoming aware of you.

- Avoid wearing brightly colored or shiny clothes.
- Keep as quiet as possible—any sound will scare the animals.
- If it's windy, place the hide so the wind is blowing toward you. This will prevent the animals from picking up your scent.
- Remain as still as you can.
- Be patient. Wildlife might not appear right away.

Use binoculars, a telescope, or a camera with a zoom to get a close-up view of the animals.

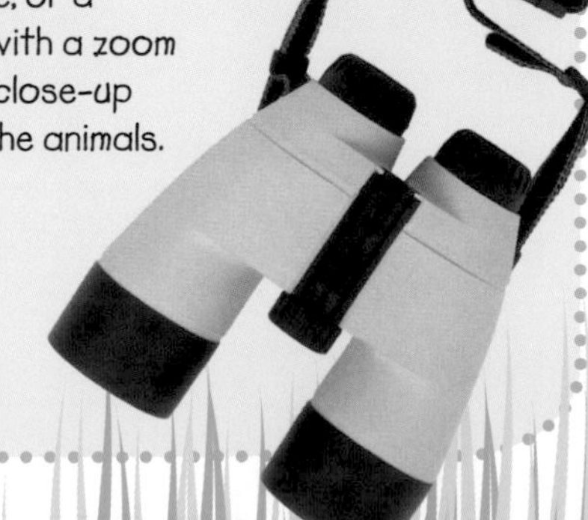

Bird-watching

Why not buy a good bird identification guide so that you'll be able to name the birds you see? Watch closely and after a while you'll be able to compare and recognize the behavior, movement, and songs of different birds.

Wren singing

Other hides

You could hang an old piece of material over a table and make a peep hole in it or, alternatively, lie on the ground and cover yourself in leaves and branches to break up the outline of your body.

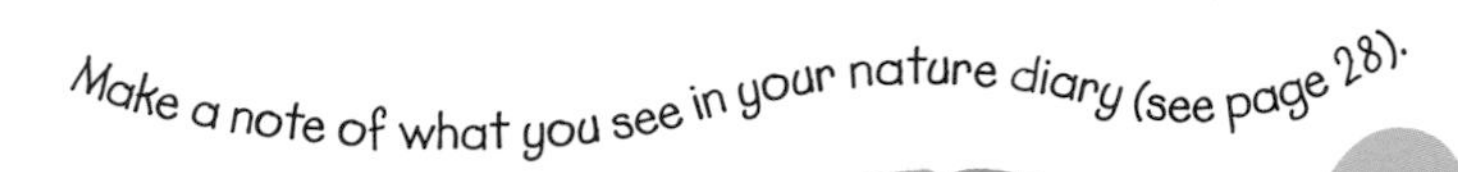

Make a note of what you see in your nature diary (see page 28).

Gray squirrel munching

How to help

If you find or spot an injured animal, watch from a distance so as not to scare it and call the ASPCA, which has the special equipment needed for handling wildlife.

Rabbit listening

Watch it

Small mammals detector

Shrews, voles, dormice, and other small mammals live in many gardens, but you will not often see these secretive creatures. They are on the hit list of many predators and move quickly to avoid being detected, but make a few of these detectors and find out if they are around.

It is very difficult to identify shrew tracks positively, since these animals are so light and fast-moving, and all you might find are blurred tracks.

Did you know?

- Shrews like to eat spiders, worms, snails, woodlice, and small insects.
- They are territorial and make high pitched shrieks if they meet another shrew.
- Shrews do not hibernate.
- Shrews live in underground tunnels or beneath rotting logs with small entrance holes.
- Shrews have to eat every 2 to 3 hours to survive.

Shrew convoy

Female shrews have up to seven young and the family is occasionally seen running along in a convoy, with the mother in front and each youngster holding onto the tail of the one in front. This mainly happens when the nest is disturbed and the mother is leading them to safety.

Long, thin tail of a wood mouse

What you will need:

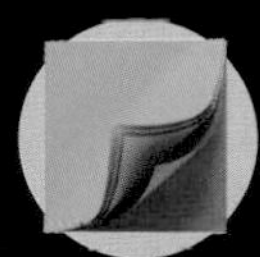

A sheet of plain paper

Two pieces of greaseproof paper, size 3x1½ in (7x4 cm) and stapler

Poster paint (nontoxic) and brush

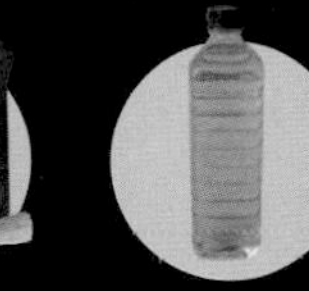

Vegetable oil

Plastic pipe, 12 in (30 cm) long 3 in (7 cm) diameter

Peanut butter and long stick

1

Staple each piece of greaseproof paper to the ends of the sheet of paper.

2

Mix the poster paint with an equal amount of vegetable oil. Brush the mixture onto both pieces of greaseproof paper.

3

Slide the paper into the pipe.

IDENTIFYING TRACKS
Mice and larger small mammals are more likely to leave behind more distinct prints than shrews.

4

Place a dollop of peanut butter on the top surface halfway down inside the pipe using a stick. This food will attract visitors.

5

Leave the tube overnight along a grass edge or a wall, or at the bottom of a hedge. In the morning, slide out the sheet to see if there are any tracks.

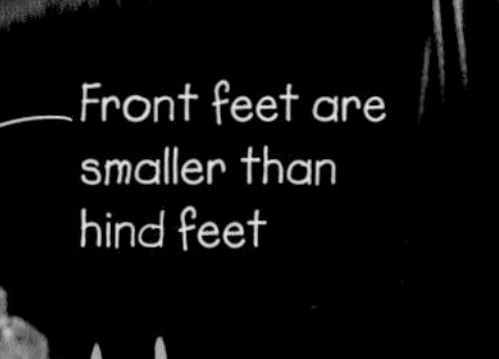

Front feet are smaller than hind feet

Make it

Night visitors tracker

Many creatures remain hidden during daylight, but when the Sun goes down they wake up and come out to hunt and gather food. You may occasionally spot a creature when you look out the window at night, but many of these animals are shy. By identifying their tracks you can find out what's been visiting your garden.

Red foxes are unfussy eaters, feeding on insects, fruits, birds, small mammals, and even our food scraps. Listen for the barks and cries of these prowlers of the night.

The furry raccoon is easily recognized by its black-and-white mask on its face. It will eat almost anything.

Animal tracks

Use this animal track guide to help you identify what kind of animals are wandering through your garden at night. Count the number of toes on the front and hind feet and look for claw marks.

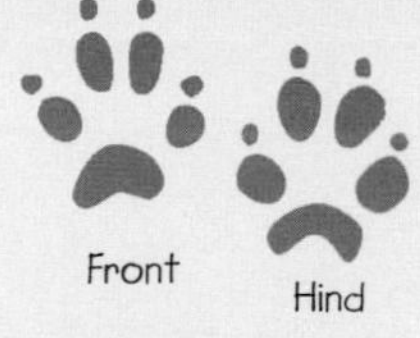

Dog family

Members of the dog family, such as foxes, walk on their toes. Their tracks show four toes in both their front and back feet with claw marks.

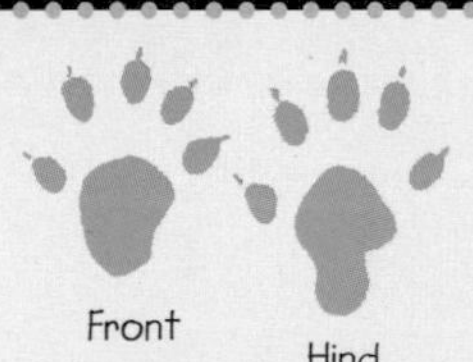

Mustelid family

Mustelids such as weasels and stoats walk with their heels flat on the ground. Their tracks have five front and hind toes with claw marks.

Cat family

Cats walk on their toes and pull in their claws so their tracks show four toes on their feet and no claw marks.

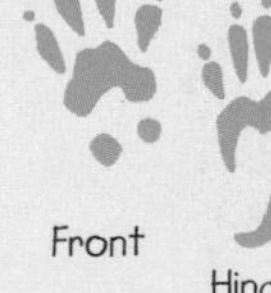

Rodent family

Mice and other rodents walk flat on their feet. The front foot has four toes and the back foot has a long pad with five toes. Their tracks also show claw marks.

Did you know?

- Many animals have features that help them find their way around at night, such as whiskers and large eyes.
- Nocturnal animals generally have a highly tuned sense of hearing and smell, which helps them to know where other creatures are located.
- Some animals have many predators and are nocturnal because the dark gives them more protection than daylight.

Virginia opossums are the only marsupial—pouched animal—living in North America. If attacked, they pretend to be dead, hoping that the predator will lose interest.

Aided by their special night-vision eyes, cats are suited to hunting at night.

Nighttime expedition

If you're feeling adventurous, wrap up warmly, take an adult and a flashlight, and venture outside into the dark—a moonlit night is best. The key to seeing nocturnal animals is to move quietly and wait patiently. Use your flashlight to find your way, but don't leave it on all the time.

What you will need:

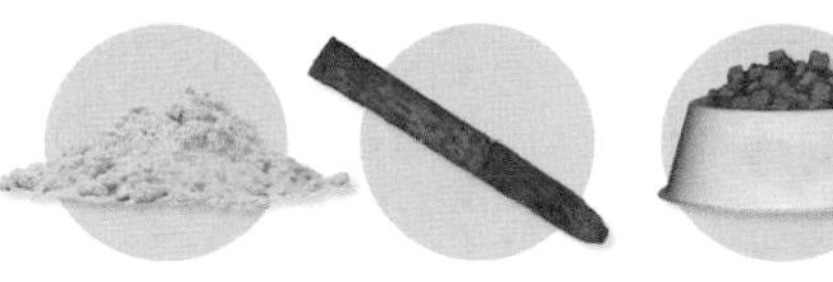

Sand   Stake   Dog food and saucer

1 **Cover an area with sand** and smooth out using a stake.

2 **Put some dog food** in the middle, making sure the sand stays pristeen.

3 **Look the next morning** for any animal tracks. Clear away the food to keep from attracting rats.

Night-scented plants

Wildlife gardening doesn't stop when it gets dark. Growing plants that smell strongly all night attracts moths and other flying insects—the perfect airborne snack for hungry bats.

1

Honeysuckle

(Lonicera periclymenum 'Serotina')

The white and purplish flowers of the honeysuckle plant smell gorgeous in late summer and fall. Honeysuckle is a climber that makes a pretty cover for a fence or wall, or when trained into the branches of a tree.

- Sunny or partly shaded location
- Moist, well drained soil
- Grows 22 ft (7 m) high

2

Evening primrose

(Oenothera biennis)

Evening primrose flowers every two years. It makes a rosette of leaves in the first year, followed by a towering flower spike the next. The large yellow petals open up in the evening, making a bowl shape and releasing a powerful scent. Delicious for moths!

- Suny location
- Well drained soil
- Grows 4 ft (1.2 m) high

3

Soapwort

(Saponaria officinalis)

You can hardly spot the green leaves of this plant. They are totally covered up by a riot of white or pink flowers. From summer to fall, you, along with nectar-drinking insects, will enjoy this beautiful floral spectacle.

- Sunny location
- Well drained soil
- Grows 24 in (60 cm) high

4

Dame's rocket

(Hesperis matronalis)

Dame's rocket's white flowers glow in the moonlight. They attract moths with their beautiful scent in the late spring and summer.

- Sunny or partly shaded location
- Moist, well drained soil
- Grows 35 in (90 cm) high

5

Valerian

(Centranthus ruber)

Thick clusters of strongly scented flowers appear from the beginning to the end of summer. Valerian are available in several colors, but choose those with white flowers to attract moths.

- Sunny location
- Well drained soil
- Grows 3 ft (1 m) high

6

Verbena

(Verbena bonariensis)

This tall, elegant perennial has wiry stems topped with tufts of purple flowers. Bees and butterflies visit them during the day, and moths come flocking at night. And where there are lots of moths… there are bats!

- Sunny location
- Moist, well drained soil
- Grows 5 ft (1.5 m) high

7

White jasmine

(Jasminum officinale)

This climber has an unmistakeable perfume, which is at its best on a warm summer's evening. Despite having such a big scent, the white flowers are only about the size of a marble, and very delicate.

- Sunny or partly shaded location
- Well drained soil
- Grows 40 ft (12 m) high

8

Phlox

(Phlox paniculata)

The white flowered forms of phlox draw moths to them like a high powered magnet. The clusters of flowers appear above bushy clumps of jagged leaves. The show of fragrant flowers can last from summer until early fall if the dead heads are removed regularly.

- Sunny or partly shaded location
- Moist soil
- Grows 4 ft (1.2 m) high

9

Flowering tobacco

(Nicotiana alata)

During the day the scent from this plant is sometimes barely noticeable, but after dark it becomes intense. Masses of yellowy green, tube-shaped flowers appear in summer and are a beacon for moths.

- Sunny or partly shaded location
- Moist, well drained soil
- Grows 5 ft (1.5 m) high

10

Night-scented stock

(Matthiola incana Brompton stocks)

This bushy plant comes in a range of colors, including pink, white, and red, but they all have one thing in common—a sensational perfume that is released by the flowers all summer long.

- Sunny location
- Moist, well drained soil
- Grows 24 in (60 cm) high

Spotting bats

The best time to see bats is at dusk, when they leave their roosts in nooks and crannies to hunt for food. Bats also prefer calm, clear evenings and don't go hunting in the cold, wind, or rain.

Bats can also be seen around lamp posts hunting the moths flying near the light.

Grow it

Bats' bog garden

Bats gobble up huge numbers of flying insects every night. Attract these insects to come and live and breed in a bog garden and you'll provide bats with a meal and help to prevent the decline of these endangered mammals.

What you will need:

2 stakes and string
Old paddling pool, deflated
Scissors
Shovel
Bog plants
Pebbles
Watering can

1 **Mark a circular area** by attaching a length of string to a stake at each end. Stick one stake in the middle and use the other to mark the ground.

2 **Dig out a hole** to the same depth as the paddling pool, using the spade. Put the mud on one side, or into a wheelbarrow, to use later.

3 **Make a well defined ledge** by patting the edge of the hole firmly all the way around.

4 **Place the paddling pool** into the hole and cut to size if necessary. Make a few small holes in the bottom for drainage. Pour the mud you dug out back in.

5 **Plan where to put** the wild, marshy flowers, then plant them in the ground. We used lychnis, acorus (sweet flag), iris, scirpus, veronica, and schizostylus (Crimson flag).

6 **Pour over a little rainwater** to make the mud moist, using the watering can. Use the pebbles to mark the edge of the bog garden.

Did you know?

- There are about 1,100 species of bat worldwide.
- One of the smallest US bats is the Eastern pipistrelle, with a wingspan of 8 in (20 cm).
- Bats can live 30 years.

AFTERCARE
Make sure the soil does not dry out. In winter, cover the soil with fallen leaves to protect delicate plants and to enrich the soil.

Bats' diet

The tiny pipistrelle has a big appetite—it can eat up to 3,000 bugs a night. Midges, mosquitoes, moths, crane flies, and spiders are all on their dinner menu.

Finding insects

Ever heard the saying "blind as a bat"? Well they're not, but they don't use their eyes to find insects. Bats use echolocation, which is similar to sonar. As they fly they make sounds and listen to the echoes. The length of time it takes for the sound to bounce back lets them know where an insect is located.

Glossary

Amphibian
An animal that can live in water and on land.

Annual
A plant that completes its whole life cycle in a year.

Arachnids
A group of invertebrates that have eight legs.

Camouflage
An animal's skin pattern, which helps to hide the animal from an enemy.

Carnivore
An animal that eats other animals.

Chrysalis
The protective casing of a pupa (a caterpillar changing into a butterfly).

Climber
A weak-stemmed plant that uses other plants or man-made structures for support as it grows.

Compost
A rich mixture of decayed plants that is added to the soil.

Conservation
The process of protecting wildlife and their habitats.

Echolocation
An animal's use of reflecting sound (echo) to locate objects.

Endangered
An animal or plant that is threatened with extinction.

Evergreen
A plant that keeps its leaves all through the year.

Fledglings
Young birds.

Forage
To search for food.

Germination
When seeds sprout and start to grow.

Habitat
A place where wildlife lives.

Hibernate
To rest over winter.

Insect
A small animal with six legs and a body that consists of a head, thorax, and abdomen.

Invertebrate
An animal without a spine.

Larva
A newly hatched wingless grub that will become an insect.

Mammal
A warm-blooded animal, whose female feeds its young with its own milk.

Native
Plants or animals that originate from your country.

Nectar
A sweet liquid produced by flowers.

Nocturnal
Active at night.

Nutrients
Food that helps plants and animals to grow.

Nymph
A larva of an insect with undeveloped wings.

Perennial
A plant that has a life cycle that lasts three or more years.

Pesticides
Chemicals used to kill animals that harm plants.

Pollinator
Wildlife that helps to fertilize a flower by transferring pollen from a stamen to a stigma.

Predator
An animal that hunts other animals for food.

Prey
An animal that is hunted by another animal.

Pupa
A larva changing into an adult insect.

Reptile
A cold-blooded scaly animal.

Rodent
A mammal that has two pairs of continuously growing front teeth.

Index

Acknowledgments

Dorling Kindersley would like to thank:

Brockwell Park Community Greenhouses
Brockwell Hall,
Lambeth,
London, UK SE24 6HX
for the use of their area, and especially to Diane Sullock one of the site supervisors for helping us to arrange this.

Diane Sullock

Will Heap, photographer
www.willheap.com

Vauxhall City Farm
Urban farm and community garden
165 Tyers Street, London, UK SE11 5HS
Director: Sharon Clouster

Models

Lizzie and Kitty Yarrow, Isobel Salt, Charlie Duffy, Max Hadley, Louis Charlish-Jackson, Brianna Hills-Wright, Fiona Lock, Hannah and Max Moore, Fiona Larman, Cara Crosby-Irons, Dillon McLaren-Keogh, Scarlet Heap, and Yegor Koldunov.

We would also like to thank Sara and Peter Yarrow for Whitebarns location and Furneux Pelham C. of E. School and Marlborough First and Middle School, UK.

Picture credits

The publisher would like to thank the following for their kind permission to reproduce their photographs:

(Key: a-above; b-below/bottom; c-center; f-far; l-left; r-right; t-top)
Alamy Images: Arco Images GmbH 13tr, 19b, 42c (eggs); Arco Images GmbH/ Delpho, M. 10bl; Robert Ashton/Massive Pixels 42cb; Tim Ayers1 69cr; Pat Bennett 3tr, 19tr, 30bl (blue butterfly); Dave Bevan 1; blickwinkel 7cr, 41r, 42c (larvae), 70tr; Blickwinkel/Schmidbauer 75cla; Nigel Cattlin 22br, 42c (adult ladybug), 49cl; David Chapman 17l; Judith Collins 10clb (hedge), 11crb (hedge); Ashley Cooper 37br; Derek Croucher 3fbr, 52tl; Andrew Darrington 42c (pupa), 75fcra (moth); Andrew Digby 65br; Emil Enchev 75br; floralpik 38tr; Robert Harding Picture Library Ltd 10-11t, 30-31cb (blue sky); Steffen Hauser/botanikfoto 39bl; Janice Hazeldine 17c; Skip Higgins of Raskal Photography 31cl; Bob Jensen 30clb (swallowtail butterfly); Keith Leighton 38br; Darren Matthews 30cb (butterfly feeding); Chris Mattison 59br; Malcolm Muir 10cl (red admiral butterfly); Nature Picture Library 52cl; Mike Read 32cra; Helene Rogers 76ca (paddling pool); Scenics & Science 50br, 51c; David Tipling 7bl; Natural Visions 13tc; Wildlife GmbH 75clb; Wildpictures 52crb; Wildscape 50tr; Kathy Wright 38tc; **Ardea**: Pascal Goetgheluck 43br; **Richard Carter, www.gruts.com:** 6clb; **Julie A. Craves:** 40c; **F. Deschandol & Ph. Sabine**: 45tl, 45tl (pupa); **DK Images**: Dorling Kindersley © Geoff Dann 21crb (cypress hedge); Frank Greenaway © Dorling Kindersley, Courtesy of the Natural History Museum, London 2cla, 30cl (monarch butterfly), 34bl, 36tr, 46tr; Stephen Hayward 24l; Dorling Kindersley © Josef Hlasek 20br, 21cl; Colin Keates © Dorling Kindersley, Courtesy of the Natural History Museum, London 10clb (moth), 31br (moths), 37ca, 37cr, 37cra, 37tc, 37tl, 37tr, 57ca, 77cr, 77cra; Kim Taylor 17ca, 21cra; Cyril Laubscher © Dorling Kindersley 60tl; Natural History Museum, London 16tr; Dorling Kindersley © Rollin Verlinde 21br; James Young 19cra; Jerry Young 31clb (ladybugs), 42cl, 50tl, 57cla, 63br; **Keith Durnford, www. img66.com** : 70tl; **FLPA**: Leo Batten 54tr; Cisca Castelijns/Foto Natura 32crb; Nigel Cattlin 38bl; Robin Chittenden 55tl; Alan & Linda Detrick 74ca; Michael Durham/ Minden Pictures 74tr; Tony Hamblin 12-13c; John Hawkins 16l; Willem Kolvoort/Foto Natura 55tr; Rene Krekels/Foto Natura/Minden 58bc, 58bl (baby newt); S & D & K Maslowski 66fbr, 67cl; Rosemary Mayer 13cb, 20-21 (background hedge); Phil McLean 43tr, 69br; Derek Middleton 59crb, 70b; Hans Schouten/Foto Natura 55tc; Malcolm Schuyl 75tl (moth); Mark Sisson 6cla; Gary K. Smith 32ca; Jurgen & Christine Sohns 55bc; Mike J Thomas 51tr; **Paul Fly**: 74cb; **D Friel** : 20cra; **Getty Images**: 9tr, 15crb, 16r, 19crb, 20cb, 26crb (chrysanthemums), 26crb (fuschia), 29br, 30-31b (grass), 37c, 59cr, 67bl, 73ftr; **Leslie Hebdon**: 38bc; **Marshal Hedin**: 47tl; **Alex Martin, scotia10, http://www.flickr.com/photos/97041038@N00/**: 75ca; **Julie Hucke**: 39tl; **Isadore Berg, http://www.flickr.com/photos/isadoreberg/**: 77t; **iStockphoto.com**: 25br, 51b; Robert Harnden 74bl; Jon Horton 47br; proxyminder 68ftr (butterfly); **Gale Jolly**: 3ftr, 10cla, 10clb, 22tr, 24br; **Keven Law, http://www.flickr.com/ photos/66164549@N00/**: 6br; **LinderRox, http://www.flickr.com/photos/ linderrox/**: 25tr (seedlings); **Bruce McAdam**: 23l; **naturepl.com**: Jose B. Ruiz 32l; Nigel Bean 12cra; Dave Bevan 58fbl; Philippe Clement 74clb; Georgette Douwing 50cr; Chris Gomersall 12crb; Kim Taylor 45ftr, 45tr, 50crb; Steve Knell 15tr, 58br; Willem Kolvoort 54tl; William Osborn 65tr; Michel Poinsignon 12cb; Colin Varndell 67tl; John Waters 6tr; Dave Watts 55bl; **NHPA/Photoshot**: Laurie Campbell 69t; Stephen Dalton 59tr; **Photolibrary**: 15br, 54tc, 61bl; Garden Picture Library/Howard Rice 74cla; Garden Picture Library/Jerry Pavia 13clb; Garden Picture Library/Linda Burgess 12ca; Garden Picture Library/Michele Lamontagne 75cra; Garden Picture Library/Pernilla Bergdahl 74crb; **Science Photo Library**: Andy Harmer 52bl, 52clb; John Sanford 72 (moon); John Walsh 52br; **Rachel Scopes**: 29t; **Aubrey James Shepherd**: 21bl; **D. M. Shreeve**: 5l, 7r; **Jim Thatcher, http://www.flickr.com/photos/jimthatcher/**: 60cr; **Cara Tytler**: 15cra; **ukstormchaser**: 21tc; **Eddy Van Leuven**: 2bl; **Nicolas J. Vereecken**: 40bc, 40bl, 40br; **S Evelyn Vincent**: 54bl; **Martin Werker** : 61r; **Christopher L. Wood, Albany, USA, www.flickr.com/photos/orodreth_99**: 38tl

Jacket images: *Front*: **DK Images**: Jerry Young fcra (beetle), ftr (bee); **Getty Images:** Amana Images / Marie Dubrac / Anyone ftl; DK Stock / David Deas fbl; STOCK4B c; **Photolibrary**: Foodpix fcla.
Back: **Corbis:** Jorma Jämsen / Zefa c; **GAP Photos**: fbr;
Getty Images: First Light / Natalie Kauffman ftr